First published in 2007 by New Holland Publishers (UK) Ltd
London • Cape Town • Sydney • Auckland
Garfield House, 86–88 Edgware Road, London W2 2EA, United Kingdom
www.newhollandpublishers.com
80 McKenzie Street, Cape Town 8001, South Africa
Unit 1, 66 Gibbes Street, Chatswood, NSW 2067, Australia
218 Lake Road, Northcote, Auckland
Copyright © 2007 text AG&G Books
Copyright © 2007 illustrations and photographs New Holland Publishers (UK) Ltd
Copyright © 2007 New Holland Publishers (UK) Ltd

ISBN 978 184537 9254
10 9 8 7 6 5 4 3 2 1

Editorial Direction: Rosemary Wilkinson Editor: Naomi Waters Production: Hema Gohil
Designed and created for New Holland by AG&G Books Copyright © 2004 "Specialist" AG&G Books
Design: Glyn Bridgewater Illustrations: Dawn Brend, Gill Bridgewater, Coral Mula and Ann Winterbotham
Editor: Alison Copland Photographs: see page 80
Reproduction by Pica Digital Pte Ltd, Singapore
Printed and bound in Malaysia by Times Offset (M) Sdn. Bhd.

P9-CDT-706

The SELF-SUFFICIENCY

Specialist

The essential guide to designing and planning for off-grid self-reliance

A. & G. Bridgewater

NEW HOLLAND

Contents

Author's foreword **2**

Author's foreword

We were warned. We knew that we were poisoning our environment, so it had to happen. Our once green and bounteous Mother Earth is sick. This is not a hidden sickness; the physical symptoms are clear for all of us to see. The air is thick with pollution, our forests are shrinking, carbon emissions are rising, global warning is a measurable fact, our food contains so much rubbish that it is making us ill, the fish are dying, ocean levels are rising and there is climate chaos. The good news is that self-sufficiency offers exciting, dynamic, practical, down-to-earth solutions to the problem of how to live in a leaner, greener, cleaner way. No more sitting around being a victim and complaining about how the problem is so monumental that it can only be solved by people in power.

Self-sufficiency offers practical and detailed solutions to the problems of living in a way that will invigorate the planet. Imagine an off-grid home independent of mains services, clean wholesome organic food, fresh air, growing your own produce, more exercise, less pollution, you and your children working and playing in a world humming with healthy wildlife. Self-sufficiency offers you a real, practical, pioneering, hands-on way forward.

Measurements

Both metric and imperial measurements are given in this book – for example, 1.8 m (6 ft).

SEASONS

Throughout this book, advice is given about seasonal tasks. Because of global and even regional variations in climate and temperature, the four main seasons have been used, with each subdivided into 'early', 'mid-' and 'late' – for example, early spring, mid-spring and late spring. These 12 divisions of the year can be applied to the appropriate calendar months in your local area, if you find this helps.

What is self-sufficiency?

Self-sufficiency is an eco-friendly way of living that involves being self-contained in terms of energy, food and shelter. To put it another way, if you grow your own organic food, keep some livestock, cut back on your use of electricity and fossil fuels (natural gas, petroleum and coal), if you store away your produce, and generally spend a good part of your time working on the land, then you are well on the way to being self-sufficient.

What will it involve?

QUESTIONS TO ASK YOURSELF

You may have dreamed about going self-sufficient but how do you put your ideas into practice? The following list of questions may help towards planning for a self-sufficient lifestyle that is tailored to your needs.

LIFESTYLE

- Do you want your self-sufficient lifestyle to be an all-encompassing philosophy for living – something that touches every aspect of your life – or are you simply going to change some aspects for the better?
- Do you want to change everything at a stroke, or are you going for a little-by-little approach?
- If you have a partner – and this is of vital importance – is she/he totally with you on this?
- Do you want your particular dream plot to be in the city or in the country?
- Can you make your dream happen by staying in your present home and renting fields and allotments?
- Do you want a smallholding of, say, half a hectare (around 1 acre) or a hectare (around 2 acres)?
- Are you going to try to be organic?
- Are you going to try to be eco-green in all things – housing, food, clothing, possessions?
- Do you want to put all your time into self-sufficiency, or are you going to opt for a compromise and work for, say, half the week to supplement your needs?
- Do you either need or want to completely change your career for one that backs up and/or makes your self-sufficiency possible?
- Could you perhaps sell up your city home and use the money to buy a home in a less expensive area, such as the countryside or abroad?
- Could you join forces with like-minded people – friends, family or a commune?

FOOD

- Are you aiming for a traditional smallholding set-up with, say, chickens for meat and eggs, a cow or goat for meat, milk and cheese, and crops to feed you and the stock?
- Are you a vegetarian, and if so how will this impact on your lifestyle?
- Are you going to try to be organic?
- Are you going to attempt to be completely self-sufficient in food?

A small wind turbine will produce enough electricity to light the average home with 3–4 bedrooms.

ENERGY

- Are you aiming to go off-grid and do without mains water, gas and electricity?
- Are you going to look to the past and manage without electricity? Or are you going to look to the future and go for high-tech solutions?
- Are you going to have a wind turbine?
- Are you going to have a geothermal plant?
- Are you going to super-insulate your home?
- Are you going to give up your car in favour of some other transport, or perhaps downgrade your present vehicle for something less fuel-guzzling?
- Are you going to have a borehole or well?

ANIMALS

- Are you going to keep livestock such as chickens, pigs or bees?
- If you are not going to keep stock, how will you nourish your land?
- Are you going to keep the stock primarily for your food – eggs, milk and meat – or do you want to sell any surplus?
- Do you have enough space for stock?
- If you are aiming to keep stock (say a cow for milk), have you considered the implications – feeding, animal welfare, milking, 24-hour care?

The benefits of self-sufficiency

What is in it for me?

The benefits are so all-encompassing that they will touch every aspect of your life. You will eat better food, with no chemicals, preservatives, taste enhancers, artificial colours, herbicides or pesticides. You will feel more in tune with nature. You will use less (non-renewable) fossil fuel. Your fuel bills will go down, your stress levels will go down, and generally you will be living a healthier, more exciting, more enriched, more satisfying and more caring life.

ENERGY SAVINGS

One look at the average home will demonstrate that not only are most of us incredibly greedy in terms of energy – we want bigger homes, bigger vehicles, bigger appetites, bigger everything – but, even more illogically, a good part of the energy that we do use is wasted. Our homes and lives are leaking energy at every seam. If we did no more than look at self-sufficiency from a very narrow money-saving viewpoint, it is pretty obvious that most of us could quite easily and dramatically reduce our spending on energy, simply by bunging up a few of the leaks.

If we look carefully at our spending – heating, cooling, lighting, water, waste, transport and so on – and then apply the self-sufficiency mantra 'little in and little out', it is plain to see that the best way forward would be to minutely examine our energy needs, and see if we can attack the problem from both ends – meaning reduce both the initial need and the resultant waste. It would be wonderful if we could afford to make huge dramatic high-cost changes, but for most of us the best way of saving energy is to make lots of small modifications. You should not try to change everything at a stroke, either; it is much better to tackle one problem – say lighting – and then to move on to the next one.

So, for example, we could all cut our heating costs at a stroke simply by wearing more clothes, having thicker curtains, settling for a slightly lower level of heating, and living a more active lifestyle. Of course, this advice is rather simplistic, but I am sure you get the point.

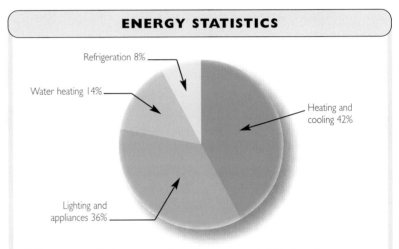

ENERGY STATISTICS

Refrigeration 8%

Water heating 14%

Heating and cooling 42%

Lighting and appliances 36%

↗ Energy costs will of course vary depending upon your individual needs.

- **Insulation** – Every household spends about 42 per cent of its energy budget on heating and cooling. In the knowledge that most of this energy leaks through the structure of the house, we could make huge savings simply by insulating our homes.
- **Wind turbines** – Every household spends about 36 per cent of its energy budget on lighting and small appliances. If every household did no more than fit a very small, low-cost 1 kW turbine, use energy-efficient light bulbs, and reduce lighting to a sensible level, then lighting bills could be halved.
- **Geothermal energy** – When it comes to geothermal energy, it is very difficult to quantify savings. All we can say is that, in terms of coefficient of performance (meaning how much energy is used set against how much energy is produced), while a fuel like coal is about 70–90 per cent efficient, geothermal energy is 400 per cent efficient. Even if we discount these figures as being wildly exaggerated and settle for geothermal energy as being twice as efficient as, say, coal and gas energy, then heating/cooling costs could be halved.
- **Solar energy** – There are so many options with solar energy – passive heating and cooling, solar collectors heating water, solar photovoltaic cells producing electricity, and so on – that really it is almost impossible to say that any particular way is best. Nevertheless, if we brought together passive insulation and passive solar gain, we could at the very least halve our energy costs.

THE ENVIRONMENT

The average person in a developed country throws away about 450 kg (1,000 lb) of rubbish every year. The easiest way for us to make a difference to the amount of energy used and the amount of pollution produced would be to cut both consumption and waste. If we buy fewer throwaway items – short-life goods and packaging – and if we recycle goods, we will take weight off both ends of the consumption-pollution seesaw. With efficiency and conservation being key components of energy sustainability, the best advice for us as individuals is to tackle the problem by nibbling away at our initial need for grid energy. The truth is that if we all did a little the problem would be well on the way to being solved.

Many people who are new to self-sufficiency find it difficult to stay focused and balanced. For example, I know of one couple who are doing their best to be self-sufficient; they keep chickens for eggs and bees for honey, they grow fruit, they run courses, and so on. Yet, while they are so desperately concerned about every aspect of the environment – cars, fossil fuels, organic food – their neighbours drive huge, fuel-guzzling cars, and are champions of unrestrained consumption. The question is what to do? The answer is beautifully simple. We live in a free society where each one of us is entitled to do what we like within the law. These neighbours are perfectly entitled to lead their lives as they think fit. My advice to this young couple would be to quietly lead their own lives – certainly they should not preach or in any way start telling the neighbours how they should lead their lives. The best that they can hope for is that things will slowly change around them – smaller cars, incentives to recycle rubbish, and so on.

ORGANIC FOOD

Even the most ardent anti-organic growers and producers – those people and organizations who were once pulling up hedges, spreading artificial fertilizers and spraying chemicals and pesticides everywhere – are now coming around to the fact that the future has to be organic. The reason for this huge U-turn on the part of governments is that, for growers who once advocated factory farming, facts, figures and reports have shown that the dangers of agrochemicals and pesticides are all too real. The endless food scares have shown that 'what goes around comes around'. The simple fact is that, if we spread poisons on the land today, these self-same poisons will be back on our plates tomorrow.

All that said, while we do have to look at the negatives in farming – if only to see how not to do it – it is so much more exciting and upbeat to look at the positives. Perhaps it is enough to say that, from a self-sufficiency viewpoint, organic gardening and organic food can be equated with tastier food, healthier eating, more exercise, improved nutrition, a healthier environment, better soil conditions, better wildlife and geneally a healthier lifestyle.

Home-grown organic food is the best option on many counts – it is tastier, healthier and all-round good fun to grow.

LIFESTYLE

If nothing else, digging the garden will make you fitter, and you won't have trouble sleeping.

Being self-sufficient will eventually have an impact on every aspect of your life – where you live, how you live, the work you do, the car you drive, the food you eat, and all your activities. In this respect, it is very difficult to dabble with self-sufficiency, or settle for half measures. For example, it would be strange to become interested in off-grid energy and then buy a car that has a very high fuel consumption – the two just would not go together. So it is for food, entertainment, clothes, everything. Once you start out on self-sufficiency it is very difficult to be anything other than totally committed. Being committed does have its problems, and it can be hard work, but the positive aspects will by far outweigh the negative ones. You will be eating better food, your appetite will be better, your stress levels will go down, you will know what it is that you are eating, you will get more physical exercise, you will be fitter, you might well be able to give up your car, and you will be presented with a whole range of interesting food-producing options – chickens, pigs, bees, organic gardening. You may be able to say that you are physically tired and exhausted, and doing so much exercise that you are losing weight, but you will not be able to say that you are bored or stressed, or have difficulty sleeping.

Considering your options

How can I get started?

To become self-sufficient, there are many ways to begin. You could stay as you are and make lots of small modifications to your life; you could go for one massive life-changing upheaval and move house and career; you could make it work in the town, or in the countryside, or abroad. There will almost certainly be an option to suit your specific needs. There are lots of ways of reaching the same destination.

MAKING SMALL CHANGES

You could turn your garden over to producing food, change your diet, adopt different shopping habits, change the way the house is heated, change your use of electricity, gas, oil or solid fuel, change your vehicle, walk to work, only work half of the week, and so on. You could run an allotment, rent a piece of land, keep chickens and sell the eggs, or keep bees, for example.

A good solar heater will help reduce your water-heating costs.

MAKING A MAJOR CHANGE

We are all very different – different ages, and with different family and financial commitments – but in my opinion the best, and perhaps even the easiest, method of going self-sufficient is to move to a plot in the countryside. Certainly, such a major change would involve a lot of forward planning, and you would have to build in all sorts of safety nets, but it would be a great goal to aim for. Of course, you could in the mean time prepare the way by making lots of small changes as described above.

GATHERING INFORMATION

As with any great journey or scheme, it is vital that you prepare by gathering as much information as possible. You must talk to your friends and family, visit possible locations, look at your assets, talk to people who are self-sufficient. You must consider every aspect of what is possible, and then research all the implications. If you want to move to the countryside, you should have an extended visit. If you want to keep animals, you should try working on a farm. You must base your dreams and subsequent plans on good, solid, reliable information.

Questions to ask yourself

- If you do want land – how much do you need?
- Could you make it all work in the town or city, or do you need to move to the countryside where the land and property are often less expensive?
- Could you make it work by moving abroad?
- If you do have plans to move to another country, can you speak the language?
- If you have children, how will your plans affect their lives? Are they at a critical stage in their schooling?
- Do you want to go off-grid – no mains electricity, water or gas?
- Do you have practical skills in woodworking, electrics, plumbing, cooking, gardening or animal husbandry?
- Can you make it happen by staying put and renting fields and allotments?
- Do you want/need the support of a like-minded group – a community?
- Do you want/have to make a complete career change, or can you make it happen by adopting a career that backs up the self-sufficient set-up?
- Do you have enough assets to make your plans possible?
- Could you join forces with your parents, your partner's parents, friends or family? If yes, have you ever lived and/or worked together?
- If you go in with parents or friends – how will such an arrangement affect other members of the family?
- If you go in with friends, partner or family, what happens if one party wants to pull out?
- Could you form a co-operative with friends and neighbours, with you all clubbing together to buy land?
- Could you join forces with family members to purchase a good-sized country house complete with land?
- Do you want to go the whole hog – move house, grow your own food, keep livestock – or would you be content to stay put, concentrate on beekeeping perhaps, and sell your produce in order to buy in other goods and services?

GETTING DOWN TO DETAILS

Once you have decided in broad terms that you want to be in the town or the countryside, you must start looking at the fine details of what is possible. The following will point you in the right direction.

Town
- In the UK, allotments are low-cost, sometimes even free for people who are on a small income.
- Lots of allotment associations traditionally allow chickens, rabbits, goats and other stock.
- A large garden could be turned over to food production – you could have one or more greenhouses.
- You could rent ground – from neighbours, private individuals and local councils.
- Keeping livestock in town can be a problem – people will complain about smells and noise.
- Town-based self-sufficiency has to be tightly controlled because space is at a premium.
- There will be local restrictions – how many chickens, how much noise, and so on.
- You might not be allowed to have a wind turbine, but you could insulate your house and fit solar collectors.
- You will be able to draw inspiration from cultural activities such as visiting museums, art galleries and theatres and attending lectures.
- You could bring public transport into the overall equation.
- You will easily be able to do part-time paid work to support your go-green activities.
- You could sell produce like goat's milk, cheese and fresh vegetables at the garden gate.
- There are a growing number of inner-city community farms; perhaps you could join such a set-up.
- Your children will easily be able to get to school.

For some people the off-grid option complete with a wind turbine is at the heart of the dream.

Countryside
- The feeling of space can be spiritually uplifting – you will be very aware of the changing seasons.
- In the context of self-sufficiency, living in the country equates with more space, which in turn equates with more choice.
- If you have a large garden – 0.2 hectare (half an acre) or more – you will be able to keep livestock – anything from chickens through to a cow.
- Living in the country will give you greater access to tools and materials – all the things that you need to set your self-sufficiency dreams in motion.
- Noise pollution is low, which is very important. You will be able to hear yourself think, the birds singing, your animals calling, the wind in the trees, and so on.
- Light pollution is low. You will be able to see the stars at night – perfect if communing with nature is important to you.
- Land costs, meaning those of agricultural land, are low. You can rent whole fields, spreads or woods.
- Rural activities are good fun and relatively low-cost, but more importantly many of them will relate to your go-green endeavours. For example, not only will the various county shows feature old tractors, crafts and eco-products, but perhaps more importantly they might offer you an outlet for your goods or produce.
- Not only will you have room to take up horse riding, watch nature, build eccentric garden structures, run around the garden singing or whatever takes your fancy, but the space will allow you to experiment and build some of the off-grid options – such items as a wind turbine or a water turbine, in fact all sorts of large structures that you could not build in town.
- There are fewer people in the countryside. You will have more personal space, which can be very important for some people.

A large number of allotment holders are already completely self-sufficient in organic fruit and vegetables.

A place in the town

Is urban self-sufficiency feasible?

Reports suggest that there are three groups of go-greeners: those who live in the town and yearn for the countryside; those who live in the countryside and want to be even more isolated; and those who enjoy living in the town and want to stay put. There are few country people who yearn to live in the town. The town dwellers who want to stay put are at an advantage because they are already familiar with the possibilities and limitations of their environment.

A carefully chosen, well-fitted, on-house wind turbine is a good option for a town house.

An allotment will allow you to be self-sufficient in basic fruit and vegetables for the table.

Fresh herbs can be grown in containers on the patio and doorstep, as well as indoors on the windowsill.

FREQUENTLY ASKED QUESTIONS

You can turn the majority of your garden – most of your decorative beds – over to food crops.

- **Is it possible to be self-sufficient in town?** Yes, but it is very different from trying to make a go of it in the countryside. As might be expected, town-based self-sufficiency usually has more to do with the efficiency of the house, growing produce, and keeping chickens, rather than having large dynamic structures such as wind turbines, and practising large-scale animal husbandry.
- **Are allotments a viable option?** Allotments are a very good option in some countries – they are low-cost and in most of the UK there are still plenty on offer. Many allotment associations traditionally allow holders to keep small livestock such as chickens, rabbits and goats.
- **Can I turn my whole garden over to growing fruit and vegetables?** Yes, as long as you do not break any local regulations or codes. For example, while you can have one or more greenhouses, you usually cannot have a polytunnel.
- **Can I turn my garden over to livestock?** Much depends upon the size and location of your garden, but usually there is nothing to say that you cannot have small animals such as chickens or rabbits.

- **Are there any restrictions against animals?** Most local-authority restrictions concern noise, mess and smell. For example, in a town house, although you might be allowed to keep chickens, pigs might be off limits.
- **Do I need to ask permission from the neighbours?** For the most part, your neighbours will not mind what you are doing, as long as it does not impinge upon their space. However, while most people are happy with chickens, rabbits and perhaps even a couple of goats, some people have a real fear of bees.
- **Do I need permission for a wind turbine?** Much depends on the size of your garden and the type of wind turbine, but the answer is generally yes – you do need permission from your local authority. Wind turbines are becoming smaller and more compact, however, and government thinking is rapidly changing, so keep a check.
- **Do I need permission for a solar collector?** The rules vary depending upon precisely where you live, but, although you do need permission from your local authority, it is generally given. Once again, as governments are now giving grants to encourage off-grid energy, the likelihood is that you will get permission.

A place in the country

How is rural living different?

Certainly, a country person will know more about country life than a town person, but the inspired town dweller who wants to follow the dream and move to the country is likely to be very strongly motivated. While a town person might be completely ignorant of all the complex and sometimes harsh realities of country living, this in itself can put them at an advantage. Sometimes it is good to look at a problem from a fresh perspective.

Your first fresh, straight-from-the-hen egg will be a joy!

Beekeeping is a good option; it is relatively low in cost, you will be able to join a local group, and there is always a ready market for local honey.

A good-sized polytunnel will allow you to extend the growing season for the greater part of the year – planting a month or two earlier and harvesting a month or two later.

Sheep are a good low-cost option, but your children may make friends with the lambs.

FREQUENTLY ASKED QUESTIONS

- **Is a country option easier?** It is easier in the sense that there is more space, but not so easy in terms of travel and transport. I think that country living is by far the easiest go-green option because land is often less expensive, there is more space, and there is more choice.
- **Is a country life lonely?** Living in the country can be quite lonely, especially if you are seen as being different. Living in a small community can be very restricting as everyone will know your business. If you are of an independent nature, you will feel empowered. Certainly, there are fewer people, but you will have more personal space – a very important factor for some people. Then again, country people can be very caring and protective. If you have school-age children, you will soon be drawn into school and village activities.
- **Is transport a problem?** Transport costs can be high, especially if you live off the beaten track. You will need a reliable van or truck – possibly a four-wheel drive (try to choose a fuel-efficient model).
- **Is livestock a difficult option?** Livestock needs year-round care, even on celebration days. If you have a cold, flu or a sprained ankle, it can be a huge problem. However, while some people see animals as a tie, others see them as an opportunity to de-stress and be more in touch with nature.
- **Is the countryside as romantic as it sounds?** Yes, the feeling of space, the ever-changing seasons, the animal life, the silence, the birds singing, the wind in the trees – the country can be spiritually uplifting. The other side of this coin is that the physical realities of country living can also sometimes be harsh, cruel and relentless.
- **Is there less pollution in the country?** There are fewer car fumes and factory smells, and noise and light pollution are low, but some farmers still use some nasty chemical sprays and dips, and country roads can be noisy and busy.
- **Is it possible to buy land?** Yes, agricultural land – a small field, small wood or patch of scrubby land – is generally low-cost and readily available. That said, you can easily rent fields, spreads and woods.
- **Is the weather in the country different?** The weather is not in any way better or worse, but in the country it makes more of an impact. Whereas adverse weather in the town can make things a bit difficult – the paths a bit wet, the trains running slowly – the same weather in the country can bring everything to a standstill.
- **Will my children have things to do?** If your kids want to build a camp in the fields, climb trees, ride horses or join the village youth club, that is great. Rural activities can be good fun and cheap. On the other hand, they might, to some extent, miss out on visits to the cinema and such like. This needs thinking about.

The reality of keeping livestock for food production will at some point have to be faced.

A good-sized piece of land will allow you to have a large wind turbine that will produce all or most of your electricity.

The self-sufficient town house

What are the main considerations?

The self-sufficient town house aims to be autonomous in terms of energy and waste, like a space capsule. It is super-insulated, and may have a solar collector for heating, a Trombe wall (see page 25), a geothermal system to convert the earth's heat into heating or air-conditioning, a wind turbine to convert the power of the wind into electricity, a recycling system for water, a kitchen garden for food, and a composter for kitchen and garden waste.

A GOOD LIFE IN THE TOWN

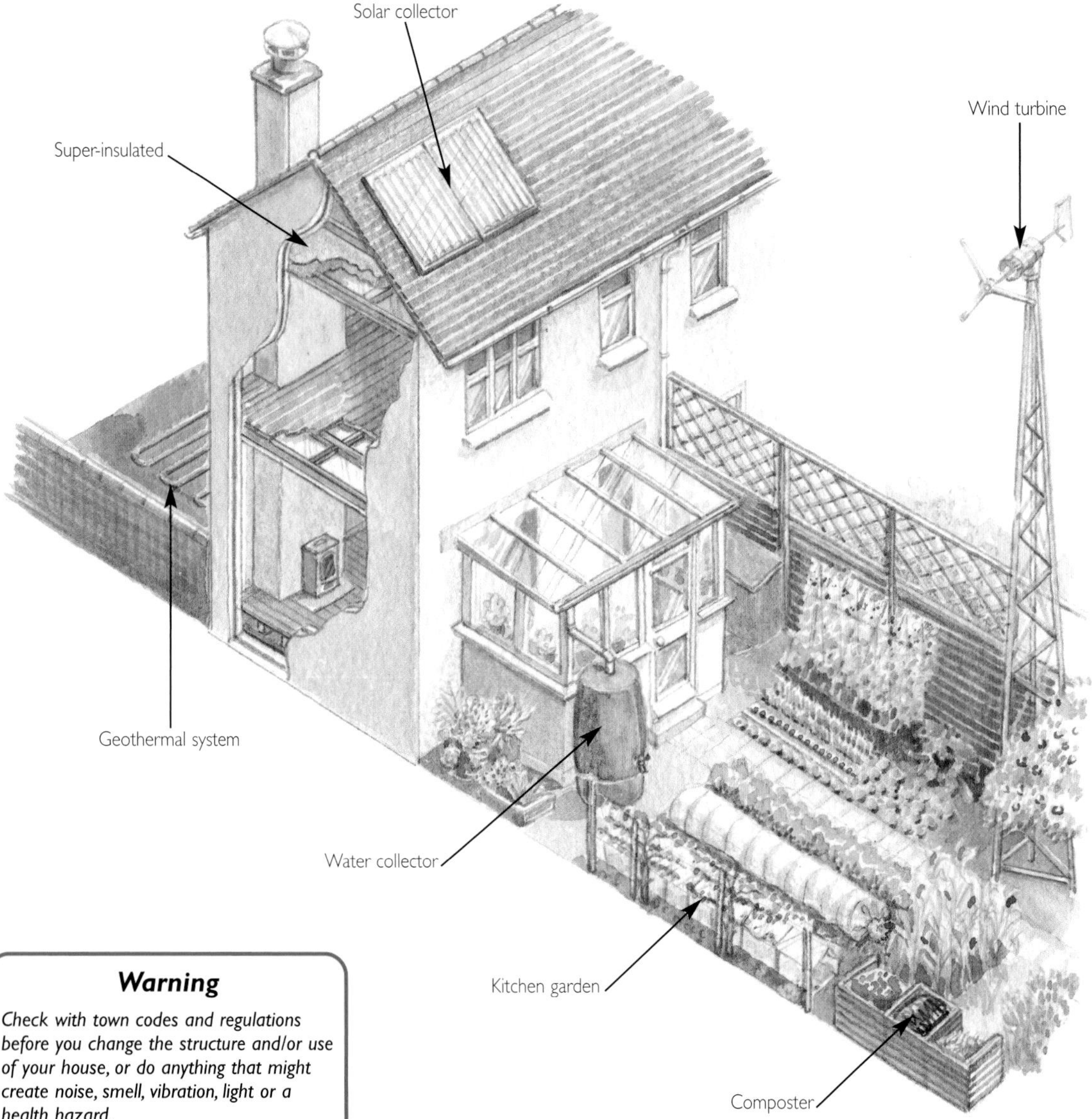

Solar collector

Wind turbine

Super-insulated

Geothermal system

Water collector

Kitchen garden

Composter

Warning

Check with town codes and regulations before you change the structure and/or use of your house, or do anything that might create noise, smell, vibration, light or a health hazard.

AN ECO-GREEN AVENUE APARTMENT BLOCK

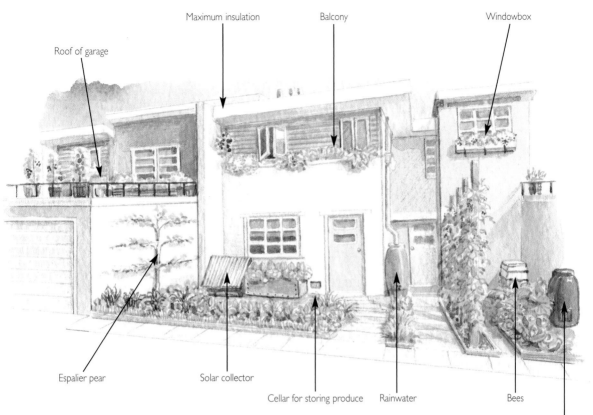

Roof of garage

Maximum insulation

Balcony

Windowbox

Espalier pear

Solar collector

Cellar for storing produce

Rainwater

Bees

Composter

OTHER AVENUES TO EXPLORE

- Could you join forces with others and between you maintain a small town house in your home country and a large rural house abroad?
- Are there local-authority or government grants for insulation, turbines, solar collectors, recycling?
- Could you join forces with neighbours and cultivate some common land, create an urban farm, rent ground from the council, or make contact with a school and set up a produce group?
- Is a small wind turbine a possibility?
- Could you share or rent a room in exchange for cash or help in the gardens, for example?
- Could you give up or share a car?
- Could you maintain one or more aged neighbours' gardens and share the resultant produce?

Self-sufficiency checklist

- Have you maximized the insulation in the walls, the roof and the floor space?
- Have you cut down on the use of energy-guzzling appliances?
- Are you composting or recycling all your kitchen and garden waste?
- Are you using every scrap of outside space for growing produce – flower borders, lawns, balconies, the roof of the house, the garage roof, windowboxes, cellars, allotment, even the neighbours' garden?
- Is there room for livestock such as chickens, bees, rabbits or a goat?
- Have you fitted a solar collector on the roof or in the garden?
- Have you fitted photovoltaic cells on the roof?
- Are you collecting the rainwater and/or making use of 'grey water'?
- Have you talked to your neighbours and made sure they are happy with your plans?
- If you live in a semi-detached property, remember that, to a greater or lesser extent, you jointly own the roof, fences, garden and view with your neighbour. This being so, have you made sure that all parties are happy?
- Some new property developments are designed to be eco-friendly and near self-sufficient in energy. Have you considered buying one of these?

The self-sufficient village cottage

The self-sufficient village cottage is much the same as the town house in that it aims to be autonomous in terms of energy and waste, but the primary difference is that the space allows for larger structures, larger gardens, and most importantly a broader range of livestock. The space also allows for a greater degree of experimentation if you want to adopt a slower approach involving recycling materials, collecting materials and creating experimental structures.

TRADITIONAL SELF-SUFFICIENT COTTAGE

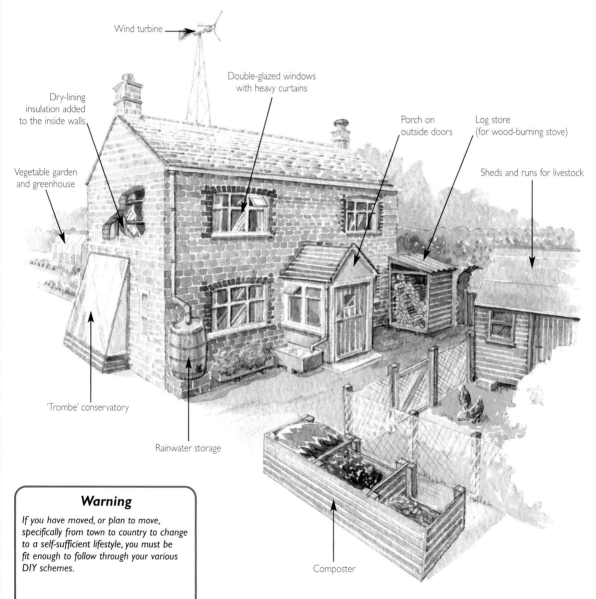

Wind turbine

Double-glazed windows with heavy curtains

Dry-lining insulation added to the inside walls

Porch on outside doors

Log store (for wood-burning stove)

Vegetable garden and greenhouse

Sheds and runs for livestock

'Trombe' conservatory

Rainwater storage

Composter

Warning

If you have moved, or plan to move, specifically from town to country to change to a self-sufficient lifestyle, you must be fit enough to follow through your various DIY schemes.

A BEAUTIFUL AND TASTY COTTAGE GARDEN

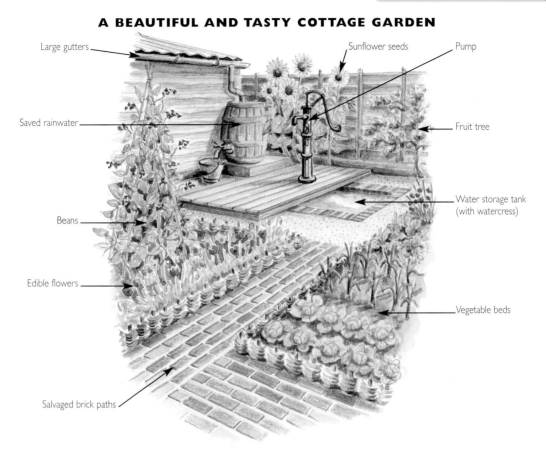

Large gutters

Sunflower seeds

Pump

Saved rainwater

Fruit tree

Beans

Water storage tank (with watercress)

Edible flowers

Vegetable beds

Salvaged brick paths

Self-sufficiency checklist

- Have you fitted heavy curtains and/or shutters to all windows and exterior doors?
- Do you open the curtains during the day and close them at night to keep the heat in, and do you wear layers of clothes when the weather is cold?
- Have you replaced all single-pane windows with double- or even triple-glazed units, or at least covered existing glass with plastic film?
- Have you reduced the number of exterior doors?
- Have you insulated the roof space and all cavity walls, or, if you have solid walls, have you added insulation to the inside or outside surfaces?
- If you live in the northern hemisphere, have you reduced the number and/or size of north-facing windows, and increased the size and number of south-facing windows – and vice versa if you live in the southern hemisphere?
- Have you installed a wood-burning stove, and removed items like gas/electric fires?
- Have you fitted vents and ducts to channel excess heat around the house?
- Have you fitted glass porches or conservatories over exterior doors, and fitted vents at floor and ceiling level to direct rising hot air from the glass structures into the house?
- Have you fitted solar collectors on your roof to pre-heat water for cooking, heating and bathing?
- Have you modified the water system to save and reuse grey water, so you can flush the toilets with recycled water?

OTHER AVENUES TO EXPLORE

- You could change the layout of the rooms and fit a central log-burning stove, so that the whole family can sit around a central fire.
- You could fit fences and/or plant hedges on the windward side of the garden.
- You could fit a wind turbine.
- You could rent land.
- You could put the greater part of your garden into food production.
- You could try your hand at keeping livestock by making contact with local farmers and seeing if they would be willing to show you some of the ropes.
- You could learn a craft or skill such as bee- or pig-keeping, spinning, tractor maintenance – a skill that is completely outside your experience.
- You could stop using your TV, radio, washing machine, fridge and power tools to see what it feels like, and to reduce your power costs.

The self-sufficient smallholding

What is a smallholding?

A self-sufficient smallholding is a set-up of at least 1.2 hectares (3 acres) where all aspects of self-sufficiency have been considered and as many eco-friendly measures as possible have been implemented. A property of this size requires a high degree of investment in terms of money, enthusiasm and commitment. The space allows for a large vegetable garden, livestock, areas given over to animal food crops, and all manner of off-grid systems.

SELF-CONTAINED AUTONOMOUS HOUSE

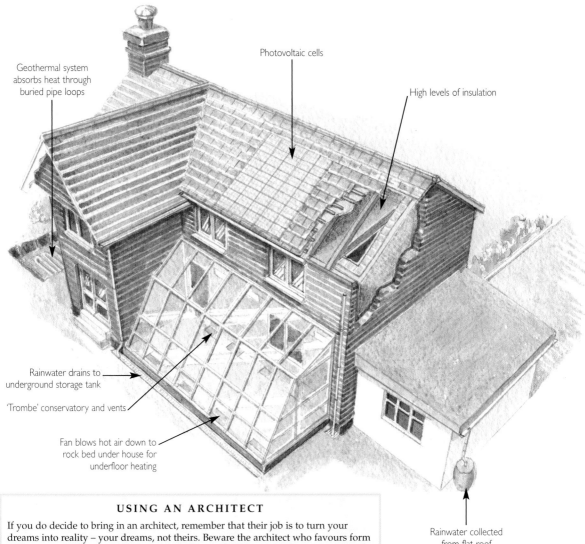

Geothermal system absorbs heat through buried pipe loops

Photovoltaic cells

High levels of insulation

Rainwater drains to underground storage tank

'Trombe' conservatory and vents

Fan blows hot air down to rock bed under house for underfloor heating

Rainwater collected from flat roof

USING AN ARCHITECT

If you do decide to bring in an architect, remember that their job is to turn your dreams into reality – your dreams, not theirs. Beware the architect who favours form at the expense of function. You need an architect who knows about eco-systems, off-grid systems, passive heating systems, total insulation, natural materials, Trombe walls (see page 25) and so on.

SMALLHOLDING FARM

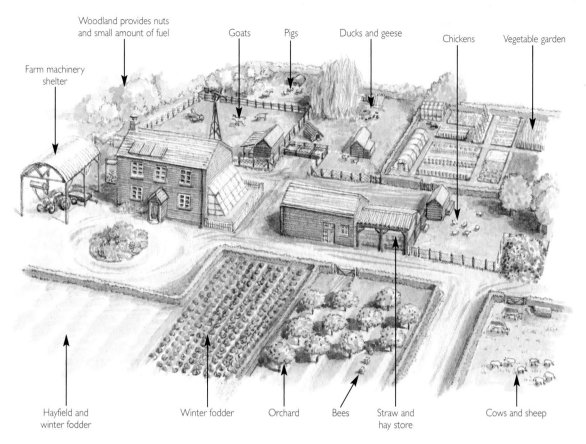

Woodland provides nuts and small amount of fuel

Goats

Pigs

Ducks and geese

Chickens

Vegetable garden

Farm machinery shelter

Hayfield and winter fodder

Winter fodder

Orchard

Bees

Straw and hay store

Cows and sheep

Self-sufficiency checklist

- If you employ an architect, does he/she understand about your self-sufficiency needs?

- Are you aiming to go totally off-grid?

- Bearing in mind that a smallholding of this size is capable of feeding a family, are you prepared, capable and fit enough to run it?

- Do you have enough capital and expertise to build the infrastructure – including fences, sheds and barns?

- Have you worked out an integrated plan that takes everything into account? For example, if you have a cow, two pigs and half a dozen sheep, are you going to grow enough feed to last them through the winter?

- Will you need a tractor with its related implements such as trailer, front loader, shredder and mower?

- Are there enough pairs of hands?

- Are you aiming to be totally self-sufficient in food, or are you aiming to concentrate your efforts on, say, milking and then raise cash by selling the surplus?

- Are you aiming to be completely organic?

- If you are aiming to put all your energies into being self-sufficient in food – vegetables, eggs, milk, fruit and meat – how are you going raise money to pay for things like tractor fuel, postage stamps, new tyres and government taxes?

OTHER AVENUES TO EXPLORE

- You could promote your self-sufficiency ideas, and raise cash at the same time, by having open days for schoolchildren and other interested groups.
- You could set part of your land aside as a wildlife sanctuary.
- You could have rare breeds of sheep or pigs, for example.
- You could rent additional land.
- You could raise money by extending one of your interests – for example, if you have an interest in old tractors, by restoring and selling tractors.
- You could give up on the combustion engine and use horses.
- You could run a bed-and-breakfast operation to bring in money.
- You could make and then sell items that utilize your produce, such as cheese, fleece, herbs, dried flowers or sheep hurdles.

Off-grid water

The term 'grid' refers to the network of mains utilities (gas, electricity and water). 'Off-grid' water is taken directly from a well, borehole or spring, or is saved rainwater. Although there is no actual shortage of water in most developed countries, the supplies of on-grid water are less certain, owing to increasing usage, and costs are constantly rising. An 'off-gridder' is a person who goes off-grid, and a 'plug-puller' someone who cuts themselves off from the grid.

WELLS AND BOREHOLES

Wells

A new-build, traditional type of well, about 9–15 m (30–50 ft) deep, is now a very expensive option. So, if you already have such a well, (better still if is brick-lined and does not run dry), you just might have a good supply of water. While the water from a 'shallow' or 'deep' traditional well ('shallow' being a well whose source of supply comes from surface water, and 'deep' being a well whose source comes from an impervious bed found beneath a porous one at a greater depth) might be cool and tasty, it can also be dangerously polluted and unreliable during periods of drought. Such water must be tested for purity.

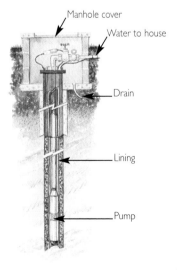

Controls

Water to house

Drain

Pump

Boreholes

A borehole is a hole about 15–30 cm (6–12 in) in diameter that has been drilled to a depth of at least 50 m (160 ft). The depth is such that it is defined as a 'deep' well, meaning the water comes from an impervious bed found beneath a porous one. Nowadays, well-boring is carried out by specialist firms who are required by Health Authorities to follow carefully set-out guidelines. This is a really good option if it strikes water. The hole is lined with a steel or plastic tube, and topped with a pump. Figures suggest that in the UK the initial cost of a borehole can be recovered in less than three years.

Manhole cover

Water to house

Drain

Lining

Pump

STORED RAINWATER

A domestic stored rainwater system (see opposite page) might be anything from a collection of water butts to a massive underground storage tank complete with filters, automotive floats and pressure pumps. Much depends on where you live, your water needs and the amount of rainfall, but a good-sized domestic rainwater system (usually called something like a 'rainwater harvesting system') can be a totally reliable and cost-effective system.

SPRING WATER

This is water that percolates through porous earth until it reaches an impervious stratum on top of which it collects. If the underlying bed is U-shaped, the water will be forced up to the highest level of the 'U', resulting in pure water that gushes or trickles out of the ground.

GREY WATER

All the water from the bath, shower, kitchen and laundry – meaning any water that is free from faeces, urine or decomposing food matter – is known as 'grey water', and it makes up about 50 per cent of the total water that we put down the drain. Figures suggest that, if we did no more than use this water to flush our toilets, we could save 50 per cent of total consumption. While there are high-tec ways of filtering grey water so that it can be reused inside the house, the easiest option is to store it and use it for watering the garden, and for various low-specification tasks such as washing the car, washing windows, or washing tools and equipment. You could also increase the usage options by reducing your use of soaps, scents and detergents.

ABOVE-GROUND COLLECTION SYSTEMS

Basic system

A basic rainwater collection system can be as simple as an underwater storage tank with catchment pipes and filters at one end, and a pump at the other. The collected rainwater can be used variously in the form of silver water – meaning it can be used for everything bar drinking, or it can be run through filters and used for everything including drinking, or it can be used as grey water for flushing the toilets.

Water storage tank

Advanced system buried to one side of the house

An advanced rainwater collection system – typically described as a 'rainwater harvesting' system – is usually a very sophisticated arrangement that involves one or more large underground storage tanks, a range of physical and ultraviolet filters, and one or more pressurized delivery outlets. Such a system sounds complex, but really it is no more than a huge version of the old Victorian kitchen system where rainwater was hand-pumped into the top of a stoneware jar where it filtered down through a silver impregnated filter tube and into a lower chamber.

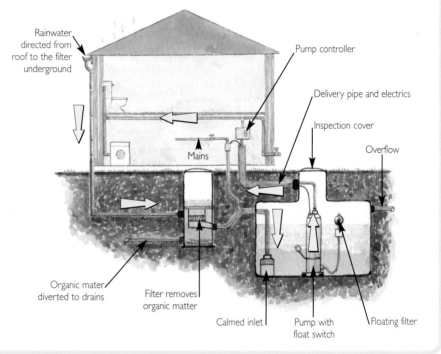

Rainwater directed from roof to the filter underground

Pump controller

Delivery pipe and electrics

Inspection cover

Overflow

Mains

Organic matter diverted to drains

Filter removes organic matter

Calmed inlet

Pump with float switch

Floating filter

FREQUENTLY ASKED QUESTIONS

- **Can I get all my water from rainwater?** We – two adults and two children – managed for ten years using nothing more than collected rainwater. We were careful, and we did our laundry in town, and we sometimes took our bathwater from a well, but it was fine. You *must* filter or boil drinking water and any water that you will use to clean your teeth.
- **Can we use the water from our old well?** The trouble with old wells is that sometimes the water comes from surface water that is to some degree polluted by animals, manured farmland, industrial waste, or even sewage. You *must* have the water tested.

- **Will a drilling company always strike water?** A good drilling company will look at all the available maps and charts, and employ a water diviner, but even then some holes are dry. You need to discuss all the possible outcomes and their consequences before you sign an agreement.
- **Will I still pay water taxes when we are off-grid?** Much depends upon where you live. For the most part, you will not pay a tax. That said some countries/areas will ask you to pay a nominal waste water tax – their argument being that your waste water will find its way to the nearest river and so consequently still need to be cleaned up.

Recycling water

Why recycle water?

In the early twentieth century, people had to use buckets to fetch water from the well. It was such back-breaking work that they tried to use as little as possible – about two buckets per day per person for everything. Nowadays, we use water for flushing toilets, baths and showers, washing machines, dishwashers, watering the garden and so on. So, while not so long ago people managed with two buckets a day, we now each use a staggering 30–60 buckets!

WHAT IS GREY WATER?

'Grey water' is a term used to describe all the domestic water from the bath, shower, kitchen and laundry – almost everything bar what goes down the toilet or bidet. The usefulness of grey water is decided by its soap, detergent and chemical content.

WHY SHOULD I USE GREY WATER?

Grey water makes up about 50 per cent of the total water that we put down the drain. If we assume that it does not make sense to flush our toilets and water our gardens with pure drinking water, it follows that, if we did no more than reuse half of the grey water to operate our toilets and water the garden, then we would save a quarter of our total water costs, and save precious water at the same time.

WHAT CAN I USE GREY WATER FOR?

Although grey water is polluted with soaps and detergents, it can still be used for tasks like flushing the toilet, washing the car and, to a limited extent, watering the garden. There are two ways you can treat grey water so that it is fit for garden use: run it through a basic or a sophisticated recycling system (see right).

HOW CAN I COLLECT GREY WATER?

You can buy a very neat, low-cost set-up to fit on top of low-level toilet systems that collects and uses the hand-wash water to flush the toilet (see page 21). The easiest option, however, is to set up a basic recycling system (see right) to divert the grey water and use it to irrigate the garden.

BASIC RECYCLING SYSTEM

A good, basic, low-cost option for using grey water from sinks, dishwasher, washing machine, bath and shower is to divert it so that it runs through a carefully organized configuration of underground leaching pipes directly to various parts of the garden. In this way, the water can be used for subsurface irrigation without you or the plants coming into contact with potentially dangerous disease-causing organisms. The proviso is that the water must not come into direct contact with fruit or salad leaves, and it must not contain too much salt.

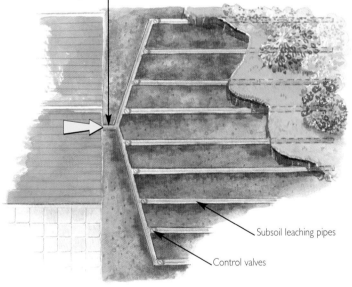

Grey water from house

Subsoil leaching pipes

Control valves

SOLVENTS, CHEMICALS AND PHARMACEUTICAL PRODUCTS

When all the left-over solvents, chemicals and drugs are put down the toilet or down the drain, their chemical components can cause long-term damaging effects on people, animals and plants. The best advice is to resist using them in the first place, or failing that to seal them in containers and take them to your local waste-management facility.

SOPHISTICATED RECYCLING SYSTEM

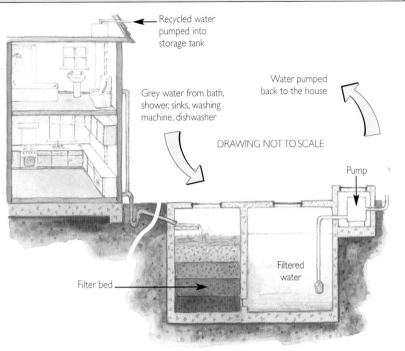

You can build a sophisticated recycling system where the grey water runs through various sand filters and into a holding tank, from where it can be used for tasks like flushing the toilet, washing clothes, cleaning the car, and surface irrigation of the garden. While such a system will clean all but the 'black water' – meaning waste water that has been contaminated with human excrement – the down side is that it is costly in terms of money and space. However, if you live in a very dry area, where water is a rare and precious commodity, the scheme might be well worth considering.

Recycled water pumped into storage tank

Water pumped back to the house

Grey water from bath, shower, sinks, washing machine, dishwasher

DRAWING NOT TO SCALE

Pump

Filter bed

Filtered water

AN INGENIOUS SINK-OVER-TOILET INVENTION

You use the toilet, make a flush, and then wash your hands. Your hand-wash water then drains into the toilet cistern. The next person uses the toilet, makes a flush using your hand-wash water, washes their hands, and so on.

You may be wondering what would happen if the person before you should fail to wash their hands – would it still flush? Not only is there a fail-safe action that tops up the water, but the whole notion of the design is such that, in a family home, most users feel compelled to wash their hands.

Sink for washing hands

Grey water goes into cistern and is used to flush the toilet

IMPROVING THE QUALITY OF GREY WATER

The main problem with running grey water through a subsurface leaching system to water, say, the roots of trees and some parts of the vegetable garden is that some detergents (especially those used in the dishwasher) are very high in salt, and of course most plants cannot tolerate salty water. In this context, you can dramatically improve the quality of the grey water simply by managing what goes down the drain. A good rule of thumb when using detergents is 'if you can't put it on your skin, you can't put it on the plants, and you shouldn't put it down the drain'.

Cautionary note

In some parts of the world, there are very strict rules when it comes to storing and using grey water. If you intend doing any more than running it through subsurface leaching pipes, you should seek advice from your local authorities.

Cookers and stoves

Can I cook off-grid?

Off-grid cooking is something of a problem, because you need a lot of heat and you need it fast. The choice is either to have a stove powered by bottled gas, oil, coal or biofuel (usually wood) from a sustainable source, or to stay with one of the traditional on-grid or fossil-fuel options (electricity, gas, oil or coal), and maximize its efficiency by using a wind, geothermal or solar system to pre-heat your cooking water.

COOKER OPTIONS

Wood-burning stove

A modern wood-burning stove is a wonderful traditional option – really good if you live near a rural wooded area and are attracted by the hands-on activity of chopping and sawing wood. In many parts of the world, wood is a first-choice fuel. Certainly, wood-burning involves a lot of physical effort, it is messy, it requires storage, and it is anything but instant, but modern wood-burning stoves are efficient, relatively low-cost, and attractive in their own right. Modern wood-burning stoves are surprisingly efficient. For example, while we burn 20–30 good-sized logs every day, we only have to empty the small, easily managed ash pan once a week. Unlike the ash from a coal-burning stove, wood ash can be used to enrich the garden. From a feel-good point of view, there is a lot of pleasure to be had from simply sitting around an oven stove and watching the flames.

↗ A wood-burning stove can become the focal point of a room.

Biofuel cooking stove

Biofuel, sometimes described as biomass fuel, is any fuel that derives from recently living organisms or their metabolic by-products. Biofuels include such materials as wood, dung, grain alcohol, crop wastes like straw, stalks and chaff, food waste. Anything that was once recently living can be turned into a liquid, solid or gaseous fuel. While wood-burning cookers are common enough, there are also cookers that run on biofuels such as green diesel, sawdust and hay bales.

If you are considering running your existing cooker on biofuel, a good way forward is to make contact with the manufacturer to find out what they advise. There are specialists who are prepared to modify cookers so that they can be safely run on biofuels. Another good option would be to research local suppliers of biofuels and ask for their advice.

↗ Many traditional stoves can be converted to run on biofuels.

FLUE OPTIONS

Back-vented stove in an open fireplace

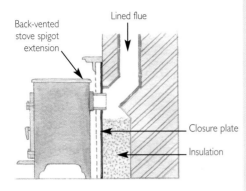

If you have a small conventional open fireplace complete with a hearth (a fireplace that is so low that you have to kneel down to look up the chimney), the best option is to have a back-vented stove, with a short length of flue that extends horizontally from the backplate directly into the fireplace opening.

Top-vented stove in a cottage-style inglenook fireplace

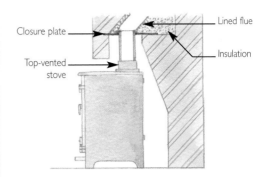

If you have a large high-level inglenook-type open fireplace (one that has an opening that is so wide and tall that you can more or less stand in it and look up the chimney), the best option is to have a top-vented stove sitting in the nook, with a short length of flue running vertically from the stove's top plate up through a metal closure plate, and on up the chimney.

Indoor flue

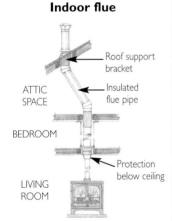

If you want to have a wood-burning stove but do not have a chimney, a good idea is to build a stainless-steel double-skin insulated flue pipe from a kit of cylindrical sections. The system allows you to run the flue up between floors without worrying about fire risks.

Outside flue

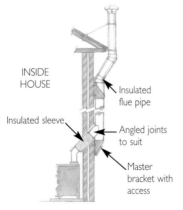

While the outside flue is much the same as the inside flue – with similar sections and specifications – the main difference is that it can be fitted without disturbing interior decorations and room layouts.

A lined and insulated chimney

Flue gases from burning wood produces tar and impurities that will in time condensate on the inside surface of the flue. Tar build-up will eventually stain your walls, run down the inside of the chimney as a sticky residue and maybe ooze onto the stove and combust, causing a chimney fire. Fitting a chimney with an insulated twin-walled liner eliminates these problems. That said, if you have kept the fire in overnight – to the extent that the viewing window is smoked and tarred up – then it is a good idea next morning to open up the various vents so that the fire roars into life and burns off the tar. If you make this 'burn-off' procedure part of your regular practice, then the flue will stay in good order.

WOOD-BURNING EMISSIONS

A modern wood-burning stove fuelled with clean forest logs produces emissions that are made up of water vapour, carbon dioxide, nitrogen, small traces of carbon monoxide, particulates and volatile organic compounds. While such emissions are also produced when fossil fuels like gas and oil are burned to produce energy, the advantage with wood is that trees in their lifetime produce oxygen and absorb carbon dioxide.

Solar collectors and Trombe walls

How can I harness the sun's heat?

There are three primary types of solar collector: a flat collector made up of an array of radiator-like pipes that sit on a thin, heat-absorbing sheet, all contained within an insulated, glazed box; a wide-angle collector made up of copper tubes complete with fins, that sits within a parabolic housing; and an evacuated-tube collector made up of a series of transparent glass tubes. Trombe walls are another method of harnessing the rays of the sun.

For optimum efficiency, the collectors must be positioned so that they point directly at the sun at midday.

In some instances, the collectors can be fixed directly to the pitched roof.

If necessary, the collectors should be fixed to frames so that they are at the correct angle.

HOW SOLAR COLLECTORS WORK

The amount of solar energy that reaches us is determined by two factors: the angle of incidence – meaning the angle at which the sunlight strikes its target – and the amount of heat absorption. Matt black absorbs more heat from the wavelengths in the spectrum than white. Solar heating systems are usually made up of five primary elements; a collector, a hot-water storage cylinder, a batch of controls and sensors, one or more pumps, and pipework. The sun heats the absorber in the collector, the heat is transferred to a fluid, a pump pushes the hot fluid to a heat exchanger in a storage tank, and the water from the storage tank is used either directly as hot water or for heating a space. Bearing in mind that the efficiency of the system hinges primarily on the collectors being mounted at the optimum angle to the sun – and this will vary depending upon your individual set-up – it is vital that you take professional advice.

It is vital that the collectors are positioned clear of overshadowing trees and structures.

TROMBE WALLS

With the Trombe wall system, the sun shines through a vertical sheet of glass and heats a masonry wall, with the effect that the space between the glass and the wall becomes a thermal chimney. Vents set at floor and ceiling level in both the glass wall and the masonry wall are opened and closed during both the day and the night so that the rising currents of hot air in the thermal chimney are variously directed in or out of the building. The system can therefore be used both to heat and to cool the building.

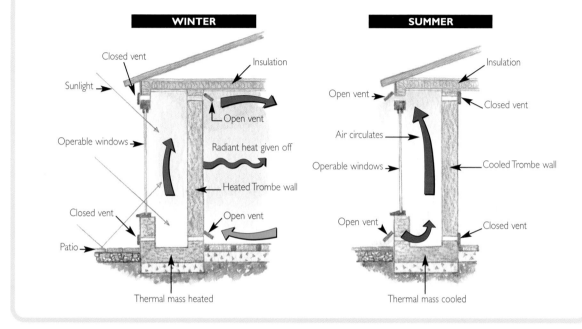

WINTER

Closed vent
Insulation
Sunlight
Open vent
Operable windows
Radiant heat given off
Heated Trombe wall
Closed vent
Open vent
Patio
Thermal mass heated

SUMMER

Insulation
Open vent
Closed vent
Air circulates
Operable windows
Cooled Trombe wall
Open vent
Closed vent
Thermal mass cooled

EVACUATED-TUBE COLLECTOR

The collector is made up of a series of transparent glass tubes that consist of an inner and outer tube, a vacuum, a heat-absorbing surface, a mirrored heat-reflecting surface and a copper heating pipe. The sun's heat is absorbed by a coating on the inner glass surface, and the heat is transferred to the tip of the heating pipe, through to a copper manifold and into the storage tank.

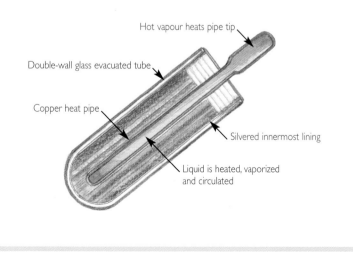

Hot vapour heats pipe tip
Double-wall glass evacuated tube
Copper heat pipe
Silvered innermost lining
Liquid is heated, vaporized and circulated

FREQUENTLY ASKED QUESTIONS

- **How does the Trombe wall system work at night?** In a hot day/cold night scenario, during the day the vents in the window are both open and the vents in the wall both closed. The hot air in the space rises by convection and passes out through the two vents at the top of the window, drawing cool air in through the bottom vent. At night, the vents in the window are closed and the vents in the wall open. The heat stored in the wall rises and passes by convection into the interior.
- **Which solar heating system do you favour?** I prefer the Trombe wall system, for the simple reason that it is low-cost, low-tech, and it does not rely on lots of sophisticated moving parts. I particularly like the notion that the sun's heat is stored within the structure of the building, and the fact that I can see and feel the system at work.

Solar or photovoltaic cells

What are these cells used for?

Photovoltaic (PV) cells are devices that convert sunlight directly into direct-current electricity. They can be used at a domestic level for lighting, and for powering low-voltage appliances such as radios, TVs, computers and small water pumps. A small PV system will only produce a few hundred watts of electricity at most, but when linked up with a battery, and when used efficiently, they will provide enough electricity for a small cottage.

Size does matter – the more photovoltaic cells you have, the more electricity they will produce.

A dual wind-sun system is a good option for operating small off-grid pumping and lighting systems.

As with solar collectors, the angle of incidence and the physical cleanness of the surface are factors that affect the efficiency of the cells.

HOW DO PHOTOVOLTAIC CELLS WORK?

Photovoltaic systems (sometimes known as PCs) work by converting sunlight into direct-current (DC) electricity. A typical PV cell structure – made up in layers – has a back contact, two silicon layers, an anti-reflecting coating, a contact grid, and an encapsulating surface. When the rays of the sun, in the form of photons, shower the structure, the resultant steady flow of electrons produces a minute amount of electricity in the form of a direct current. The amount that each cell produces is minuscule, but if you connect a whole batch of cells – in the form of, say, tiles on a roof – and use an inverter to turn DC to alternating current (AC), then you have a relatively simple and inexpensive energy source.

A STANDALONE PV SYSTEM

Standalone PV systems are designed to clip onto existing roofs. All you do is mount the panels on the roof, plug into an existing on-grid connection, and the system is ready to go. As to just how well a typical 1,000-watt system will perform in the UK, the figures suggest that it will significantly reduce your energy costs over the long term.

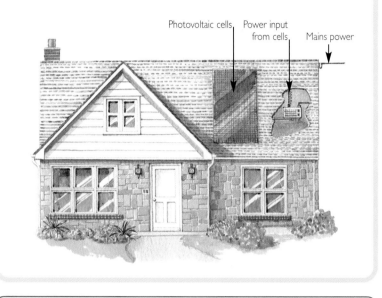

Photovoltaic cells Power input from cells Mains power

SOLAR COLLECTORS AND PV CELLS

Although photovoltaic cells are rarely seen in the UK – apart from on boats and caravans, and along motorways where they are used alongside mini wind turbines to provide small amounts of power for road signs – they are sometimes used in a small way to power solar collector systems. PV panels provide the electricity that sets the various pumps and controls in motion.

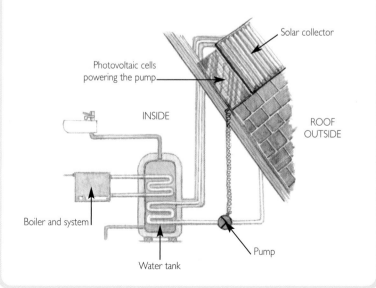

Solar collector

Photovoltaic cells powering the pump

INSIDE

ROOF OUTSIDE

Boiler and system

Water tank

Pump

FREQUENTLY ASKED QUESTIONS

- **Why is there so little interest in photovoltaics?** Apart from the fact that there is a widespread suspicion of any black-box technology where you cannot 'see the wheels turning', the design of photovoltaic cells is such that they tend to be favoured only in hot, sunny climates where there is a need for air-cooling and air-conditioning.
- **How long do photovoltaic cells last?** Manufacturers say that high-quality cells will last up to thirty years in ideal conditions. Individual cells within a panel can be replaced when they fail or if they are damaged.
- **Can a PV system be used with greenhouse rock storage?** If you have a conservatory you will know that, while it is generally warm and cosy in autumn and spring, it is uncomfortably hot in summer. A greenhouse rock storage system linked to a PV system can take advantage of this by pumping the hot air from the conservatory through to an insulated space full of rocks. At the end of the day, when there is a need for heat, the hot air from the rock store is sent by fan back to the house.

PORTABLE PV GENERATORS

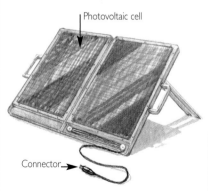

Photovoltaic cell

Connector

Portable PV generators are a good option for producing small amounts of power – for, say, a boat, a caravan or a weekend cottage. Research suggests that self-contained units of this character are finding favour simply because the user can swiftly plug them in and get on with the job.

Wind turbines

How much power do they produce?

Turbines range widely in size, and this affects how much power they generate. A small 1,000-watt wind turbine linked to a basic mains inverter will give you power for lighting plus a TV, radio and computer. If you have to go for a turbine of this size, accept the limitations and shape your other energy needs around it. For example, you could have a small turbine plus a wood-burning stove-cooker.

A small wind turbine mounted on the side of a building.

Some specialists question the practice of mounting turbines on the gable end; they say the roof will produce wind turbulence.

HOW DOES A WIND TURBINE WORK?

With a traditional windmill, the wind blows, the sails go round, and the turning action is converted by means of gears into motion – to grind corn or pump water. Most modern high-tech wind turbines have two, three or five aerofoil-section blades on the end of a horizontal shaft – a bit like an old aeroplane. With these, the wind blows, the propeller spins, the shaft turns, a generator spins and produces electricity, and finally the electricity is either stored in batteries and used off-grid, or fed directly into a on-grid tie-in system.

The ideal is to mount the turbine on a high mast so that it is clear of trees and structures.

ON-GRID TIE-IN SYSTEM

An on-grid tie-in system consists of a wind turbine mounted on a mast, a utility tie-in inverter, a bank of batteries for a back-up system, a utility switch box, and a battery-system switch box. The wind blows, the propeller spins, the horizontal shaft turns, and the generator converts the turning motion into electricity. With the tie-in system, the electricity is either used first by the house with the excess being fed back into the grid, or fed straight into the grid. Either way, such a system allows you a measure of independence.

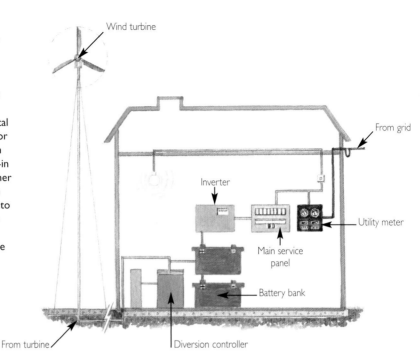

Wind turbine

From grid

Inverter

Utility meter

Main service panel

Battery bank

From turbine

Diversion controller

OFF-GRID SYSTEM

An off-grid system consists of a wind generator or turbine mounted on a tower or pole, a bank of deep-cycle-gel or carbon-fibre type batteries, and an inverter. Electricity is produced in the same way as with the tie-in system described above, but the difference is that the electricity is stored in the batteries, and then passed through an inverter and into the house as standard AC power. This is perhaps the only option for an isolated property, and/or when you simply want to go off-grid.

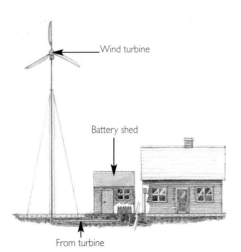

Wind turbine

Battery shed

From turbine

FREQUENTLY ASKED QUESTIONS

- **What are the size options?** They come in sizes of 600, 1,000, 1,500, 2,500 and up to 6,000 watts and more. In a three-bedroom house, a 600-watt machine will power the lights, while a 2,500-watt machine will provide enough power to run all the lights and appliances.
- **How high does the mast or tower have to be?** Heights range from 5.5 m (18 ft) for small machines right up to 15 m (50 ft) for large ones. Generally, higher masts give better air flow with minimum turbulence.
- **Can a turbine be mounted on the roof?** While there is a lot of interest in small rooftop machines, many experts in the field claim that vibrations and turbulence are always going to be a difficulty with rooftop designs.
- **Which is better – on-grid or off-grid?** For people with isolated houses and people who are aiming to cut costs to the bone, an off-grid system is the only option.

Geothermal heating

Temperatures below ground remain more or less constant, and the deeper you go the hotter it gets. A geothermal system, in the form of a buried plastic-pipe loop filled with a water-antifreeze mix, takes advantage of these constant temperatures by absorbing the heat and carrying it into the house. A system within the house extracts and compresses the absorbed heat and distributes it through the building. This process can be reversed in summer.

What does this consist of?

THE SYSTEM

The system is made up of five component parts: the heat pump, the loop of pipe, the heat-exchange liquid in the loop, the pipe or ductwork within the house, and the electricity for the various pumps. While there are, on paper, three options for the loop – it can be set in a deep borehole, underground in a pattern of trenches, or in a body of shallow water such as a lake or well – the position is usually decided by the size of the plot and/or the type of soil.

USING THE HEAT

Once the heat has been extracted from the loop, it can be used in the form of hot air or hot water. With an average system, the warm water from the loop is passed through a heat pump where the temperature is raised to about 50°C (120°F). This water can be used as domestic hot water, and/or for low-temperature heating.

EFFICIENCY

Geothermal heat pumps are rated according to their coefficient of performance (COP); in simple terms, this means according to how much energy is used set against how much energy is produced. Geothermal systems are highly efficient in that, for every unit of energy used to power the system, about four units are supplied as heat. To put it another way, while, for example, coal is about 70–90 per cent efficient, a heat pump is 400 per cent efficient. As with any other system, the best way forward is to research the options and the body of knowledge and then, in the light of the available facts and figures, pick a system that measures up to recommended standards of efficiency.

VERTICAL OR DEEP-BORE LOOP SYSTEM

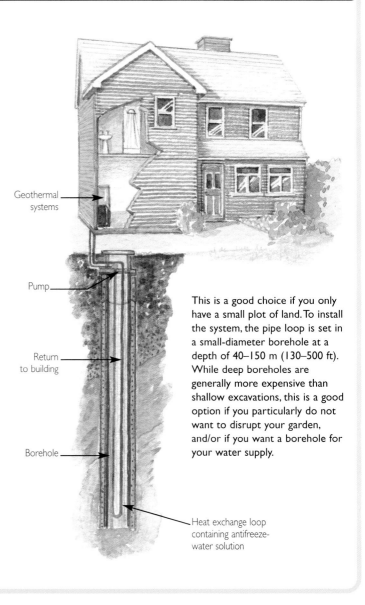

Geothermal systems

Pump

Return to building

Borehole

Heat exchange loop containing antifreeze-water solution

This is a good choice if you only have a small plot of land. To install the system, the pipe loop is set in a small-diameter borehole at a depth of 40–150 m (130–500 ft). While deep boreholes are generally more expensive than shallow excavations, this is a good option if you particularly do not want to disrupt your garden, and/or if you want a borehole for your water supply.

HORIZONTAL OR GROUND LOOP SYSTEM

Geothermal systems

Return to building

Buried heat-exchanger loop containing antifreeze-water solution

Warning

Although we say that you can cut costs by doing your own groundwork – by hiring an excavator and digging your own trenches – you should first take detailed advice from a qualified groundwork engineer.

The horizontal loop system, sometimes also called a ground loop system, is a good option if you are starting with a greenfield site and/or if you want to do the groundwork yourself. Once the system is in place, the ground can be replanted and the plants left to grow undisturbed. To install the system, bury a 100–200 m (330–660 ft) loop of plastic pipe in a trench or a block excavation of about 250–450 m² (2,700–4,850 sq. ft), at a depth of about 1.5–1.8 m (5–6 ft). This works well where the ground is firm and level, but not so well where it is rocky, marshy or unstable. Take advice if your survey indicates slippage or subsidence.

FREQUENTLY ASKED QUESTIONS

- **How can the borehole also be used for water?** Once the borehole has been drilled, two systems of pipework are put in place – a sealed loop for the thermal heating, and a single open-ended pipe complete with a submersible pump for the water.
- **Are geothermal systems high-maintenance?** The pump and compressor will need regular check-ups, but the sealed loop in the borehole or trench and the ducting or pipework are more or less maintenance-free. Most suppliers guarantee the loops for 50 years!
- **What about installation costs?** If you choose the ground loop option, and if the soil conditions are right, you could keep your costs to the minimum either by doing the groundwork yourself, or by using local low-cost labour to do it.
- **Is geothermal heating a popular option?** This depends upon where you live. It is very popular in countries where there is a shortage of fossil fuels and/or where there is a long tradition of sinking boreholes, but not popular in the UK and some parts of Europe. This situation is changing fast, however.

- **Is geothermal technology well established?** Although geothermal technology has been around for nearly 80 years, the technology has only really lifted off with the introduction of high-quality, low-cost, plastic piping.
- **Is it possible to tackle this task as a DIY project?** Much will depend on your experience and expertise, but it is possible to obtain kits. That said, it is very important that you have a ground survey carried out in order to establish the stability of your site.
- **Could I incorporate a ground loop system under my drive or tennis court?** Yes, some systems are designed to be fitted under drives, car parks and so on. A large area of black surface – like tar macadam – will increase the efficiency of the set-up.
- **Do boreholes need planning permission?** This depends upon where you live. The best advice is to make contact with your local authority.
- **Can boreholes be sited close to the house?** Being mindful that drilling a borehole is a procedure that involves a lot of mess (mud, water, noise and vibration), it is best to have the borehole drilled well away from the house.

Water or hydro turbines

Is a water turbine viable?

If you have a good-sized stream and you have the legal right to use the water, then a small turbine is an option. One manufacturer has produced a small, portable, low-cost version in which the turbine is suspended under a flow of water and wired up to a bank of batteries. If conditions are right, it will produce about 500 watts of electricity – enough for a small lighting system. If your stream is deep, narrow and fast-flowing, you could have more than one turbine.

TRADITIONAL WATERWHEELS

These need a massive body of water in the form of a mill pond, and all manner of stop/start, on/off controls such as mill races, canals, sluice gates, and so on. That said, there is no reason why an old-style wheel cannot be modified and used to drive a generator rather than to grind stones. There are still lots of companies who specialize in designing and building water turbines.

MODERN MAINSTREAM TURBINES

The most common problem is not how to use a large flow of water like a river to drive a large turbine – there is a huge choice of turbines for such a scenario – but how to use a modest stream to drive a small turbine. The easiest option here is to install a portable-type turbine. Such units are designed so that they can be dismantled into relatively manageable component parts. They work by diverting water from the stream into a holding tank, and then directing it by means of pipes through the turbine. Many well-known companies will provide small to medium-sized turbines in kit form.

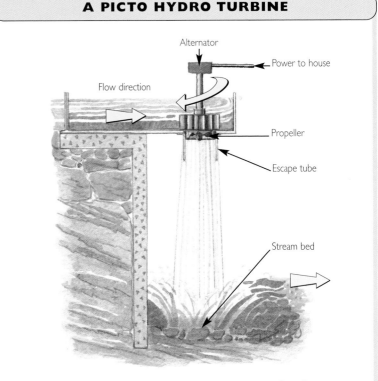

A PICTO HYDRO TURBINE

Alternator

Power to house

Flow direction

Propeller

Escape tube

Stream bed

↗ *The turbine needs a 1.5 m (5 ft) head of water and a water flow of 70 litres (15 gallons) per minute.*

FREQUENTLY ASKED QUESTIONS

- **Is it possible to cook using hydro power?** The answer is yes. The solution is to use the electricity to produce stored heat, and then use the stored heat to power a large, range-type cooker.
- **We have a river – do we have to build massive concrete groundworks?** Much depends on the flow of water, the size of the river, the structure of the soil, and so on, but generally speaking huge structures need huge ground-works. In many ways, the best option would be to go for a small turbine that can, effectively, be dangled into the water. The best way forward in this instance would be to employ a specialized company to make a detailed survey.

- **Do I have the legal right to use the water that flows across my land?** This is such a complicated issue that the only sensible advice is to start off by assuming that you do not have the right. If you begin with this premise, and then make all the necessary inquiries, you will not go wrong.
- **What is a Pelton wheel, and are they still being built?** The Pelton wheel was designed and built in 1879 in the USA by a Californian mining engineer called Lester Allan Pelton. The design involves using nozzles to jet water onto spoon-shaped buckets mounted on a wheel. Old Pelton wheels are still to be found, and modified modern versions are still being made.

Inverters and batteries

An electrical inverter changes the direct current (DC) power from a battery into the alternating current (AC) power that you need to run all the devices in your home – lights, appliances like power tools, TV, radio, computers. Connect the inverter to your bank of batteries, plug your appliances into the inverter, and you have power. You must decide up front precisely what you want to run, and then get the appropriate type of inverter to suit your needs.

What is an inverter?

BATTERIES

To store relatively small amounts of electrical energy, produced by wind turbines or hydro turbines, the best option is to use deep-cycle lead acid batteries. Deep-cycle batteries are designed to be repeatedly discharged down by as much as 80 per cent – just what you need when you are repeatedly charging and discharging. There are three types of lead acid batteries – wet or flooded batteries (as used in cars), absorbed glass mat batteries, and gel batteries. While all three types have much the same characteristics, the gel batteries are good in that they are reliable, maintenance-free, sealed, do not give off acid vapours, and unaffected by wet conditions. Do not use ordinary car-type batteries, as they simply will not be up to the task.

WARNING

Batteries are potentially dangerous – they are heavy, they can leak acid, and they can give an electric shock. Batteries must always be contained in a dry, secure, lockable shed.

BATTERY SET-UP

The diagrams show two options – a 12-volt single-battery set-up and a 24-volt two-battery set-up – both with a regulator to keep the voltage to between 12 and 15, and a dump load in the form of lights or a heater to ensure that the turbine is always running under load and therefore not overcharged. The regulator keeps your batteries up to charge, and then when the need arises diverts the extra power to the dump.

12V set-up

Turbine
Diversion load regulator
Sensor wires
Positive power
50A fuse
Single 12V battery
Resistive dump load (heater or lights)
Negative connection

24V set-up

Two 12V batteries

FREQUENTLY ASKED QUESTIONS

- **How long will a battery last?** While much depends on the type of battery and the way you use it, a top-quality deep-cycle gel battery will last anywhere from four to eight years. Batteries age badly if they get too hot, are left unused, are overcharging, or are heavily discharged.
- **What does 'thick plate' mean?** The thickness of the lead plates equates with the life of the battery – the thicker the plates, the longer the battery is likely to last. It is best to go for thick plates.
- **What does 'a cycle life rating' mean?** A battery 'cycle' is one complete discharge and recharge. This way of rating is flawed, in that, while one user might take out a lot and

another a little, both batteries will be described as having gone through one cycle. With the number of cycles being equated with just how long that battery will last, it is plain to see that a light-discharge battery is likely to last longer than a heavy-discharge one.
- **Can I mix new and old batteries?** The short answer is yes – they will still work – but the chances are that the performance of the new battery will be pulled down to match the old. For this reason, it is best to use batteries all of the same age, either all new or all old. That said, if you have the money, fully research your specific needs and start by using a bank of top-quality new batteries.

Super-insulating your home

Is insulation really that important?

Heating and cooling our homes accounts for about three-quarters of our energy costs. In an older-style, totally uninsulated house, at least 75 per cent of the heat is lost – 25 per cent through the ceiling and roof, 35 per cent through the walls, and 15 per cent through the floor. Therefore, if you maximize the insulation in your home, you can cut your energy bills by up to 75 per cent. Of all the energy-saving strategies, insulation is the most cost-effective.

REMEDIAL INSULATION

Drapes/hangings on cold walls

Draft excluders

Rugs to insulate floor

Thick curtains for windows and doors

Battens fixed to inside walls

Insulation added to inside walls

Vapour barrier

Plasterboard and wood covering

INSULATION CHECKLIST

✔ Increase the thickness of insulation in the roof space.

✔ Fit thick curtains at windows and doors – they are many times more efficient than double glazing.

✔ Make and fit draught excluders for the doors – sausage shapes stuffed with old clothes, for example.

✔ Fit plastic film insulation on the window glass.

✔ Wear appropriate clothes, all made from natural fibres – wool in winter, cotton and linen in summer.

✔ Hang decorative hangings and drapes on cold interior walls, such as patchworks, quilts, rag rugs – anything to increase the insulation.

✔ Fit more floor carpets and rugs; perhaps have layers of ethnic/folk rugs on the floors.

✔ Make a four-poster bed or a cupboard bed with curtains and drapes all around.

✔ Make and position screens between where you sit in the evening and the outside doors.

HIGH-TECH INSULATED HOUSE

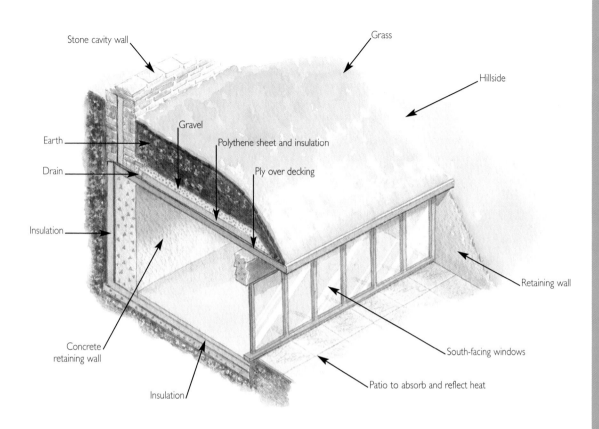

Stone cavity wall

Grass

Hillside

Earth

Gravel

Polythene sheet and insulation

Drain

Ply over decking

Insulation

Concrete
retaining wall

Insulation

Retaining wall

South-facing windows

Patio to absorb and reflect heat

FREQUENTLY ASKED QUESTIONS

- **What is an R-value?** The quality of the insulation – meaning its thermal resistance – is rated in terms of 'R'; the better the insulation, the higher the R-value. High R-values = low heat loss = low energy consumption = minimum costs = saving on global energy resources = all good.
- **How can I insulate if I am short of cash?** Start by stuffing the roof space with insulation. Later, when money allows, batten the walls, fit insulation between the battens, cover with a vapour barrier, and finally finish with plasterboard or tongue-and groove wood.
- **How can I insulate my timber-frame, tile-hung house?** Working from the inside, stuff the cavity with insulation and refit new plasterboard. Working from the outside, remove the tiles and battens, stuff the cavity full of insulation, and fit a breather membrane, vertical battens, cross battens and tiles.
- **How can I insulate my weatherboard cottage?** From the outside, remove the weatherboard, stuff the cavity with sheep's wool insulation, fit a breather membrane and new boarding. From the inside, fit counter-battens over the plasterboard, then high-tech foil-bubble-foil or more sheep's wool; top off with tongue-and groove boarding.

Bunkers and grass-roofed houses

A well-designed, semi-underground bunker house with a grass roof and windows that face the sun at midday can cut heat losses by as much as 90 per cent.

Triple and quadruple glazing

A single sheet of glass loses heat about 20 times faster than a well-insulated wall. Two sheets of glass cut the heat loss by half; three sheets halve the loss again.

Wool and hemp insulation

Sheep's fleece is a completely natural, sustainable product – non-toxic, biodegradable and altogether eco-friendly. Hemp insulation is a joy to use – it feels good to the touch, it smells good, and it is efficient. If you have bad experiences using fibreglass, then hemp is a good option.

Foil-foam-foil

Be mindful that, while foil-foam-foil insulation is incredibly efficient, with an R-value of 14.5 for a thickness of about 6 mm (¼ in), some authorities reckon that in certain situations it gives off potentially harmful gases.

Recycling your household waste

When it comes to recycling, we are big on talk and very small on action. We recycle the easy bits – about 30 per cent plastics, 80 per cent paper, and 60 per cent metal – but the greater part of our waste still goes into landfill. The environment loses out at every stage of production: fossil fuels are used, harmful emissions are created, and after a short life most products are just dumped. The best you can do is reduce your own household waste.

REDUCING WASTE

- You could just buy what you need.
- You could veto throwaway items and opt for items that can be used repeatedly.
- You could reduce the amount of packaging by buying local produce – fresh bread from a baker, fresh vegetables from a greengrocer – meaning food that does not need to be wrapped and packed for international transport.
- You could reduce the amount of waste by reusing containers and products.
- You could simply not buy products that are mostly packaging, such as canned drinks and bottled water.
- You could do your best to avoid plastic carrier bags and opt for using your own bags.
- You could try lobbying for the introduction of biodegradable options.
- You could cut back on packaging and global transport by growing your own food, and/or eating food in season.

TIPS FOR REUSING WASTE

- Burn wood as a fuel.
- Salvage wood and reuse it for DIY.
- Chip wood and turn it into garden compost.
- Turn paper and card into compost.
- Compact paper and card and use it as a fuel.
- Turn paper and card into DIY and craft items.
- Turn natural fibres – wool, cotton, silk and linen – into compost.
- Use natural fabrics – old clothes – for cleaning cloths, and compost them when you are done.
- Turn natural fibres into loft and pipe insulation.
- Turn natural fibres into craft items.
- Carefully salvage, sort and sell metals.
- Use metal for DIY.
- Turn kitchen and garden waste into compost.
- Reuse glass bottles and jars for food storage.
- Have your glass professionally crushed and use it as aggregate or decorative mulch.
- Use selected glass for craftwork.
- Use wine bottles to build garden structures such as walls or sculptures.
- Use plastic containers in the garden – mini windbreaks, plant pots, plant propagators.

An example of a well-run recycling centre that encourages us to sort our own waste.

SORTING WASTE

If you do decide to opt for putting your waste out for collection, then you could make contact with the appropriate authorities and organizations and ask them how best they would like you to present the various materials. For example, do they want you to separate the metals into types? Or do they want you to reduce the volume of cans and cartons by squashing them?

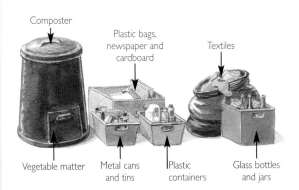

Composter

Plastic bags, newspaper and cardboard

Textiles

Vegetable matter

Metal cans and tins

Plastic containers

Glass bottles and jars

Some authorities now ask us to sort waste at the point of collection.

RECYCLING WASTE

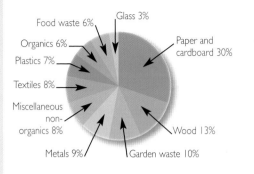

Food waste 6%
Glass 3%
Organics 6%
Paper and cardboard 30%
Plastics 7%
Textiles 8%
Miscellaneous non-organics 8%
Wood 13%
Metals 9%
Garden waste 10%

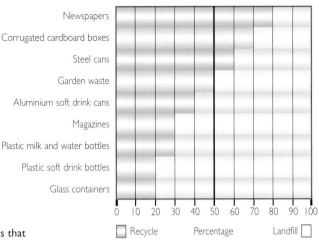

Newspapers
Corrugated cardboard boxes
Steel cans
Garden waste
Aluminium soft drink cans
Magazines
Plastic milk and water bottles
Plastic soft drink bottles
Glass containers

0 10 20 30 40 50 60 70 80 90 100

☐ Recycle   Percentage   Landfill ☐

↗ *Some authorities think our failure to recycle plastics is at the heart of our worldwide pollution problem.*

More recycling

- You could make contact with charitable organizations that make money by grading, collecting and distributing second-hand textiles.
- You could mobilize your community, and earn cash by collecting, grading and sorting paper, textiles and metals and sell them on to recycling companies.
- You could save carefully selected materials for school craft and science projects.
- You could send items like woodworking hand tools, computers and mobile phones to developing countries.

↗ *This chart nicely shows how we are still happy to dump most of our potentially toxic waste into landfill.*

Special items

Some products – batteries, household machinery, chemicals, unused prescription drugs, fluorescent strip lights, etc – need special attention and your local waste facility can advise.

PRODUCTS FROM RECYCLED WASTE

When it comes to buying products that are made from recycled waste, the market is very limited. The items are either flawed, second-rate, jokey, or in some way not right – or they are just not available. For example, while a small percentage of car tyres are turned into playground safety mulch and rubber matting, these materials are incredibly expensive and difficult to obtain. For the most part, companies tend to have little interest in recycling their products. They recycle easy and profitable sections such as paper, metal and some plastics, and that is about it.

← *A few of the everyday products manufactured from recycled materials: cardboard, bottles, cans, toilet tissue, carpet underlay, insulation, paper pulp and a garden water butt.*

FREQUENTLY ASKED QUESTIONS

- **Can we collect and sell our own household waste?** You can. Health and safety issues apart, there is nothing to say that you cannot spot an opening in the market – such as copper, lead and brass – and start collecting and selling.
- **What is the easiest option for individuals?** The easiest passive option is to boycott products. For example, you could stop using plastic bags. It is not much, but if we all did it the plastic industry would have to rethink.
- **How will growing my own food help?** Growing your own food will cut back not only on packaging, but also on the energy involved in transport. If you grow your own food and only eat food in season, there will be less global transport and less packaging.
- **Why do we have to buy disposable items?** We don't. It is still possible to opt for items that are reusable. For example, you can still use (and reuse) a paintbrush rather than a disposable roller, a cotton handkerchief rather than a tissue, or a lidded glass container rather than plastic film wrap.

Growing organic vegetables

What does organic gardening entail?

Organic gardening is a method of gardening that uses only materials that are derived from living things – meaning composts made from plants, and manure from animals. It is gardening without the use of man-made chemicals or artificial fertilizers. The mantra for organic gardening is 'Feed the soil, not the plant'. Pests are controlled by natural methods, and weeds are suppressed without the use of herbicides.

COMPOST

A compost heap nicely illustrates the self-sufficient philosophy. Kitchen and garden waste goes in at one end, time and nature work their magic, and plant and soil foods come out at the other. At least one well-managed compost heap is essential; three are even better.

TRADITIONAL SINGLE DIGGING

Divide the plot down its length. Take out one trench from the first half and put the soil on one side. Put manure or compost into the trench. Skim the weeds from the second trench into the first trench. Take out the soil from the second trench and put it over the weeds in the first trench, and so on. When you get to the end of the second half, put the contents of the first trench into the last one.

Soil from first trench is removed to the side (this fills the final trench)

FIRST HALF

SECOND HALF

Soil from first trench on second half fills last trench on first half

CROP ROTATION

Vegetables can be arranged – through their shared needs – into three groups. Therefore, divide the vegetable garden into three parts. Each part will contain one of the following groupings, which each year are rotated.

Group One

Root crops: beetroot, carrots, parsnips, salsify and scorzonera. Potatoes can also be included here.

Soil preparation: when preparing soil, neither add lime nor dig in manure. Instead, rake in a general fertilizer a couple of weeks before sowing or planting.

Group Two

Brassicas: broccoli, Brussels sprouts, cabbages, cauliflowers, kale, kohl rabi, radishes and swedes.

Soil preparation: dig the soil in winter, add well-decayed manure or garden compost, especially if the soil is lacking humus (decayed organic material, such as farmyard manure and garden compost). If the soil is acid, apply lime, but not at the same time as digging in manure or compost. About two weeks before sowing or planting, rake a general-purpose fertilizer into the soil.

Group Three

Legumes and other vegetables: aubergines (eggplants), beans, capsicums, celery, celeriac, leeks, lettuce, marrows, onions, peas, spinach, sweetcorn and tomatoes.

Soil preparation: when preparing soil in early winter, dig in garden compost or manure. Then, in late winter lime the soil (if it is acid) and, about two weeks before sowing or planting, rake in a general fertilizer.

VEGETABLE GROUPS

POTATOES Potatoes are relatively easy to grow and to store, very high in vitamin C and potassium, and an important crop.

BRASSICAS Brassicas include Brussels sprouts, kale, broccoli and cauliflower. They contain iron, calcium, vitamins C and E, and are low in fat and high in sodium.

BEETROOT FAMILY Beetroot and its 'cousins' spinach, chard, leaf beet and spinach beet are very nutritious, with no fat, few calories and lots of iron, potassium and vitamin C.

LEGUMES Legumes – runner beans, broad beans, butter beans, French bean, and peas – are low in fat, high in protein, iron and fibre, easy to grow and easy to store.

ROOTS Roots include carrots, parsnips, salsify and scorzonera; they are easy to grow and easy to store.

ONION FAMILY Onions, garlic, leeks and shallots contain the antioxidant quercetin, and they are low in calories and high in vitamins B and C.

CUCURBITS Cucurbits – marrows, courgettes, cucumbers, gherkins, pumpkins, melons and summer squashes – are a good source of beta carotene, vitamin C and folate, and are low in calories. The seeds are high in vitamin B, unsaturated fats and protein.

SALAD LEAVES Salad leaves include chicory, endive, lettuce, chives, land cress, lamb's lettuce, and some of the herbs; they are all good.

STEM VEGETABLES The term 'stem vegetables' is used to describe vegetables like celery, celeriac, asparagus and kohlrabi.

SOWING AND PLANTING METHODS

SOWING SMALL SEEDS IN OPEN GROUND
- Break the soil down into a fine, crumbly texture.
- Use a string line to mark the planting position.
- Use a hoe to make a drill to suit your chosen seeds.
- Moisten the soil and 'dribble' seed into the drill.
- Cover the seeds with soil and tamp it level.

SOWING MEDIUM SEEDS IN OPEN GROUND
- Use a string line to mark the planting position.
- Use a hoe to cut a shallow trench to suit your seeds.
- Moisten the soil and place each seed in position.
- Rake soil over the seeds and tamp it level.

SOWING LARGE SEEDS IN OPEN GROUND
- Break the soil down into a fine, crumbly texture.
- Use a string line to mark the planting position.
- Use a rake to firm the ground.
- Moisten the soil.
- Use a dibber (dibble) to make holes to suit your seeds.
- Drop the seeds into the holes, water them, and cover with soil.

SOWING SEEDS IN CELLULAR TRAYS (FLATS)
- Fill the cellular tray (flat) with a suitable growing medium or compost.
- Use a batten to skim away the excess, and firm the compost.
- Moisten the compost, sow 1–2 seeds in each cell, and lightly cover them with compost.
- When the seedlings are established, ease them out with the block of compost intact, and plant out.

SOWING SEEDS IN PEAT POTS
- Fill the peat pot with the appropriate growing medium or compost.
- Moisten the compost and firm it.
- Dib (dibble) a hole, and sow 1–2 seeds in place.
- Cover the seeds with compost and lightly water them.
- When the seedlings are up, thin out the weaker plant.
- When the seedling is well established, plant the whole seedling pot in its final position. The pot will biodegrade over time.

ORGANIC NO-DIG RAISED-BED CULTIVATION

The no-dig raised-bed method is an organic technique that involves leaving the base soil undisturbed, the idea being that fewer weeds are brought to the surface. Small raised beds are prepared, the base soil is covered with a sheet mulch – something like paper or card – the mulch is covered with a thick layer of well-rotted manure, and finally it is all topped with a mix of earth and straw, hay or woodchip.

GROWING OPTIONS

🢇 *A greenhouse is the traditional option for a medium-sized garden; there are lots of designs to choose from. A polytunnel is a good choice when you want to do your outdoor gardening 'indoors'. While there are lots of shapes and sizes to choose from, the wide and high options give the best headroom, growing space, access and ventilation.*

🢅 *Pots, containers and growing bags are a good choice if you are short of space.*

🢅 *Cold frames and hotbeds are the traditional answer to growing plants under cover. A hotbed is a cold frame that has been super-insulated with hay and manure. The manure breaks down and releases heat.*

Growing organic fruit

All fruit is good – it is tasty and nutritious, it can be eaten raw, and it is wonderfully attractive – but home-grown, organic fruit is uniquely special. Fruit in all its juicy beauty has to be the ultimate in perfectly packaged, 'convenience' food. As for choice, taste and texture, there is nothing in the shop-bought fruit market to beat a piece of home-grown fruit such as a crisp apple or a succulent strawberry.

Why grow organic fruit?

BRIEF FRUIT FACTS

- **Apples** – there are hundreds of varieties of apple.
- **Apricots** – like a mild climate.
- **Blackberries** – can be grown almost anywhere you like.
- **Blackcurrants** – are usually made into jam or jelly.
- **Cherries** – cherry trees are hardy.
- **Cranberries** – enjoy growing in boggy marsh conditions.
- **Figs** – have been cultivated since earliest times.
- **Gooseberries** – are a good, easy-to-grow choice.
- **Grapes** – outdoor grapes provide the best flavour.
- **Mulberries** – grow on fairly large trees and have a distinctive taste.
- **Peaches** – need shelter and heat.
- **Pears** – prefer a sunny, sheltered corner of the garden.
- **Plums** – are the hardiest of the 'stone' fruit.
- **Quinces** – are delicious when made into marmalade.
- **Raspberries** – are a hardy shrub of the rose family.
- **Red- and whitecurrants** – are extremely hardy.
- **Strawberries** – can easily be propagated to create more plants.

SOFT FRUIT – PRUNING AND TRAINING

→ **Blackberries:** Immediately after cutting out the fruiting canes, untie the new ones from the top wire and space them over the other wires. Leave the top wire free for young canes that will be produced in the following year. Repeat this sequence of cutting during subsequent years.

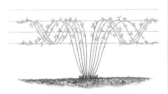

← **Gooseberries:** At the end of the season, shorten those shoots produced during that season by a half, and cut out shoots that crowd the plant's centre. Also shorten non-framework lateral shoots to about 5 cm (2 in) long.

→ **Raspberries:** During each subsequent year, in late winter cut off the tops of all canes to 15 cm (6 in) above the top of the wire. After the fruits have been picked, cut out all fruiting shoots to soil level and tie in the new canes to the supporting wires.

← **Red- and whitecurrants:** Immediately after planting, cut the main shoots back by half. This initial pruning encourages strong growth. Also cut sideshoots back to the main shoots. The illustration shows a three-year-old bush.

TOP CHOICES

APPLES Bramley Seedling: the perfect cooking apple – green-skinned and white-fleshed.

BLACKBERRIES Himalaya Giant: reliable, vigorous, late-cropping variety that produces heavy crops of large, black, high-acid fruits.

GOOSEBERRIES Leveller: reliable, yellow-green, eating/cooking variety that produces large, down-covered fruits.

PEARS Conference: popular, self-fertile, dessert variety that produces long, compact fruits.

PLUMS Victoria: the most popular and reliable, eating/cooking, self-fertile variety; it produces large crops of big, fat, firm, juicy, red-gold fruits.

STRAWBERRIES Cambridge Favourite: heavy-cropping, virus- and disease-resistant, early variety; it produces medium-sized, orange-red fruits.

TREE FRUITS FOR EASY PICKING

The three main tree fruits – apples, pears and plums – can be grown in several ways, but the simplest method for easy picking is to grow them as bushes. When grown as a bush, the plants are spaced 3.6–6 m (12–20 ft) apart, depending upon type and variety. When it comes to buying the young plants, the easiest, but slightly more expensive, option, is to get 2–3-year-old, container-grown plants from a well-established specialist nursery. Although you can plant container-grown trees out at more or less any time of the year, it is best done in winter or early spring.

ORCHARDS

Orchards are special on many counts. They are very attractive places, being full of wildlife, and a therapeutic playground for children and adults alike. They are literally very fruitful, with apples, plums and pears to eat in the hand, fruit for pies, puddings, preserves and jams, and fruit for soft drinks, wine and cider. At various times throughout the season, you can also use orchards as runs for livestock such as chickens, geese and pigs.

PLANTING A BARE-ROOTED TREE

Plant a bare-rooted deciduous tree during its dormant period, usually from late autumn to late winter. Check that the roots are not damaged; if necessary, use sharp secateurs to cut back broken and torn parts, as well as those that are thin or excessively long. Then, place the roots in a bucket of clean water for about 24 hours. If the tree was grafted, check that the union is firm and sound.

1 *Dig a hole large enough to accommodate the roots. Form and firm a mound; the old soil mark on the stem should be slightly below the level of the surrounding soil.*

2 *Knock a strong stake into the hole, so that its top is just below the lowest branch. Carefully draw friable soil over and between the roots; firm it in layers. Carefully fit a tree-tie 12–18 mm (½–¾ in) below the top of the stake. Ensure that the trunk is held secure, but not constricted. Rake the soil level and gently water the entire area.*

GROWING SYSTEMS

Espalier apples and pears

During the summer new growth will be made. Train the second tier of branches along the top wire so that they follow the same pattern as those on the bottom wire. Cut back lateral shoots from the lateral arms to three leaves above the basal cluster. Also prune back to three leaves all shoots that spring out from the central system.

Strawberry barrels

Growing strawberries in a large barrel not only creates an attractive feature, but it is a good way of making the most of a small space. The barrels can be protected with netting, snails and slugs can be controlled, and the drainage and soil within the barrel can be modified to create ideal growing conditions.

Fan-trained peaches and nectarines

During the summer choose four shoots on each arm. The first will extent the growth; two on the top side of the arm will create further arms, as will one on the underside. Cut back all other arms to leave one leaf.

Cordons

Cordons are a very good option if you are short of space. Single-stemmed trees are grown at an angle of 45° – good for apples and pears.

Outdoor grapes

Between early and mid-winter, prune lateral shoots by cutting them back to the first strong bud on the growth produced during the previous year. If the leading shoot has not reached the top wire, cut back to leave about one-third of the previous season's growth.

Growing herbs

**Why grow
herbs?**

Herbs are joy to the eye – what could be more attractive than an informal hedge of rosemary with its dark silver-green foliage and beautiful mauve flowers? Herbs are a joy to the nose – the scent of lavender is so good. Herbs are also a joy to the stomach – where would we be without mint sauce with roast lamb, and sorrel with soups and salads? If nothing else, herbs make good, wholesome but dull food better.

POPULAR HERBS

Applemint
Makes a refreshing tea

Bay
A basic ingredient of bouquet garni *and good in stews*

Borage
Makes a refreshing cold drink

Chives
Tasty in cheese dishes

Coriander
*Adds a distinct
taste to curries*

Fennel
Has a strong aniseed flavour

Garlic
*Good with a broad
range of foods*

Horseradish
Perfect with roast beef

Parsley
*Good in salads
and sandwiches*

Rosemary
Used in a wide range of foods

Sage
*Sage and onion
stuffing is wonderful!*

Thyme
*Adds a delicate flavour
to fresh grilled fish*

GROWING CYCLES OF HERBS

These are diverse and variously reflect the wide range of plant types that we think of as being herbs. They include:

- **Annuals:** single-season plants (sowing, flowering and dying all take place within the same year); these include dill, borage, marigold, coriander, basil and aniseed.
- **Biennials:** have a two-year growing cycle; these include angelica, chervil, caraway and parsley.
- **Bulbs:** swollen bases of fleshy, modified leaves tightly packed around each other; these include garlic and chives.

- **Herbaceous perennials:** long-term plants that die down to soil level in autumn and send up fresh shoots in spring; these include horseradish, tarragon, fennel, liquorice, hyssop, lovage, balm, spearmint, bergamot, marjoram, sweet cicely and sorrel.
- **Shrub-like herbs:** have a woody structure and the ability to live for many years – some are deciduous and others evergreen; these include lemon verbena, southernwood, rosemary, rue, sage and thyme.

PLANTING SCHEMES

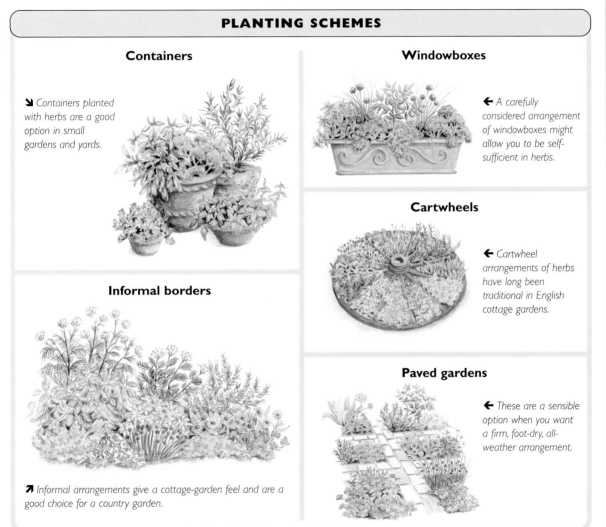

Containers

↘ *Containers planted with herbs are a good option in small gardens and yards.*

Windowboxes

← *A carefully considered arrangement of windowboxes might allow you to be self-sufficient in herbs.*

Cartwheels

← *Cartwheel arrangements of herbs have long been traditional in English cottage gardens.*

Informal borders

↗ *Informal arrangements give a cottage-garden feel and are a good choice for a country garden.*

Paved gardens

← *These are a sensible option when you want a firm, foot-dry, all-weather arrangement.*

HARVESTING

Harvest time will depend on the part of the plant to be used. Plants grown for their stems and leaves are harvested while young and before the flowers appear. Those grown for their seeds are harvested when the pods ripen. Flowers are picked at the point of opening. Herbs are best harvested in the morning, after the dew has dried, and before the sun becomes too hot.

DRYING HERBS

In the context of self-sufficiency, the best option is to use the herbs fresh or dried rather than frozen. Herbs are best dried in a well-ventilated and fairly warm place – in the larder or high up in the kitchen. When storing herbs in containers, put them in a cool, dark, dry place such as a shelf or cupboard. Label and date the containers. Carefully dried and stored herbs will retain their flavour for the best part of a year.

Keeping chickens

Are chickens easy to keep?

Chickens have long been the traditional choice for small town gardens. They recycle most of your kitchen scraps, they help keep rough grass and weeds down, and they eat lots of garden bugs and pests. You might have to feed them supplementary protein, and they do need constant care and attention, but they will give you fresh eggs for the best part of the year, as well as meat, if you are prepared to kill them. Be sure to choose a breed to suit your needs.

Chickens are a really good, easy-to-keep option for either a small town garden or a larger country garden.

CHOOSING A BREED

Buff Orpington

Plymouth Rock

Rhode Island Red

Every chicken breed has its own unique qualities and characteristics: it might be a reliable layer, lay a certain colour of egg, be hardy, be good for eating, and so on. Look at your set-up, decide on your aims – lots of big fat birds to eat, large white eggs, or whatever it might be – and then choose the breed that best suits you. The following brief listing will give you some idea of the options.

- **Buff Orpington:** large, strong, hardy, good-natured, buff- to blue/black/white-feathered, white-fleshed bird that lays brown eggs; good for both eggs and meat.
- **Plymouth Rock:** small, robust, barred white, partridge-blue-feathered, yellow-fleshed bird that is very popular in America and lays large, pink to brown eggs.
- **Rhode Island Red:** big, robust, hardy, dark brown- to red-feathered, yellow-fleshed bird that lays brown eggs; a good, reliable layer.

HOUSING OPTIONS

Walk-in shed

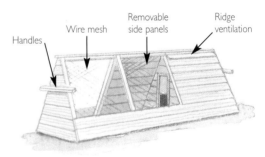

Easy access to nesting boxes

Full-height access for easy cleaning

Pop hole closed at night to keep out foxes

↗ *A traditional walk-in shed, with vents at the front, and a bank of nesting boxes; the design simplifies the tasks of cleaning and egg-collecting.*

Ark

Handles

Wire mesh

Removable side panels

Ridge ventilation

↗ *An ark with integral run; the design allows you easily to move it to a fresh patch.*

More options

There are lots of chicken houses on the market, everything from the traditional options, as shown, through to little plastic forms designed to house a couple of hens in a town garden, and walk-around sheds designed for 50 birds or more. Start by ringing your chosen area with close-mesh chicken wire. Use mesh that is about 2.4 m (8 ft) wide, and bury about 45 cm (18 in) of it in the ground, so that you finish up with a secure fence that is 1.8–2.1 m (6–7 ft) high.

FEEDING

You need a special feeder, designed to keep the food clean and dry, and a trough or low bucket for water. Apart from household and garden greens, laying hens will need grain, grit and a ready supply of either meal or layer's pellets. Greens are best hung in a net and suspended from a fence pole, so that the birds can enjoy a good feed without the greens being trodden underfoot. Layers benefit from the addition of oats and maize, while birds to fatten do well on a mix of boiled potatoes and barley meal.

Grain feeder   Net for green leaves   Sand bath

EGG PROBLEMS

Flat-sided eggs: the hen is overweight and needs to be thinned down.
Wrinkled eggs: too much starch in the diet.
Thin shells: not enough crushed oyster shell or grit in the diet.
Eggs without shells: not enough grit and/or too much protein in the diet.

Double yolks: too much spicy food in the diet and/or a genetic problem.
Blood in eggs: internal bleeding in the bird, which usually indicates a health problem.

ROUTINE CARE

What usually happens with beginners is that they get an ark, four laying birds and a supply of pellets, and they think that is all there is to it. It usually goes well for a month or so, and then the troubles begin: one bird goes off its feed, another stops laying, and so on. These problems can nearly always be solved by routine care. The water bowl must be washed daily. Every week, the house must be thoroughly swept and washed out with soapy water and disinfectant, and the birds and the house must be inspected minutely for mites. The house must also be shifted at regular intervals onto a new patch of ground.

Disinfecting

KILLING A CHICKEN FOR EATING

If you are keeping chickens for eggs and for meat, then the reality is that sooner or later you will have to kill a chicken. My advice to beginners is not to try anything yourself in the first instance, but rather to make contact with the local chicken society and ask them to give you hands-on advice.

TROUBLESHOOTING

TROUBLE	LIKELY CAUSES	POSSIBLE SOLUTIONS
Lumps on foot; the bird limps	Could be a disease called 'bumble-foot'	Wash and soak the foot in disinfectant; remove foreign materials, squeeze out pus, and dress with medication
Swollen hard crop; bird is slow-moving and droopy	Crop stuffed with long grass/fibrous plant material/feathers	Pour lukewarm soapy water into the crop to soften it up, and then massage with your fingertips to gently remove the blockage
Lots of scratching, scraggy feathers, inflamed flesh	External parasites such as red mites or lice; some mites are so small that they are difficult to see, sometimes they are so numerous they form large clusters like patches of mud	Scrub and wash the house, several times if necessary; brush and/or spray paraffin into all the cracks, corners and crannies; powder the birds and the house with a proprietary medication
In hot weather, bird looks weak	Fright/trauma. If it is very hot and more than one bird shows problems, the cause is likely to be heatstroke; if only one bird has a problem, it probably has some sort of internal rupture or haemorrhage	In the case of heatstroke, make sure that the birds are cool with plenty of water; if only one bird shows problems, keep it apart from the other birds – if the problem has not disappeared in, say, three days, then it is best to have the bird put down
The bird stands with its head erect and with its mouth gaping, as if it is gasping for breath	Almost certainly gape worms in the throat; you can sometimes see long thread-like worms in the back of the throat	Traditionally, this problem was sorted by dipping a feather in paraffin and using it to hook out the worms and to paint the throat; if more than one bird shows a problem, the ground is affected, in which case the birds need moving
Swollen joints, obviously painful	Gout and/or one of the joint diseases, or faulty feeding	Adjust the feed and talk to a vet

Keeping ducks

Are ducks easier to keep than chickens?

Ducks are slightly hardier, and therefore somewhat easier to manage, than chickens. If you have water – a lake, pond, stream or even a collection of troughs – and plenty of kitchen scraps, and you do not mind the mess they make, ducks are a good option. Because it is not easy to get a breed that is good for both meat and eggs, it is best to choose two breeds – one for eggs and the other for meat.

CHOOSING A BREED

Look at your plot and consider it in relation to ducks – whether or not it has a pond, where the land is in relationship to a water supply, how much shade it has, and so on – and then ask yourself why you want ducks rather than chickens or geese, and whether you want eggs or meat, or both. In the light of your observations, and when you have generally prepared the site appropriately, choose a breed that nicely suits your needs. The following brief list will you give you some pointers.

• **Aylesbury:** Plump, white-feathered bird considered by many to be first choice for eating; produces large, white/blue-green eggs. A good, healthy bird has glossy white plumage, a pink-white bill, dark eyes and bright orange legs and feet.

• **Indian Runner:** Good choice for rough ground; does not like to be overly confined; good for eggs, but a bit stringy for eating. There are five common colour variations – white, black, chocolate, fawn and fawn-white – the black variety has a lustrous black plumage, a black bill and black or tan legs and feet.

• **Khaki Campbell:** Khaki-feathered bird that is one of the best laying breeds, and fair for eating; a mature, healthy bird will lay up to 300 white eggs a year. The drake has a brown-shaded head, neck, stern and wing bar, and an overall khaki colour; the bill is dark green, and the legs and feet dark orange. The duck is an even khaki colour all over, with black-laced wings, a greenish-black bill, and legs and feet that match the body colour.

Aylesbury

Indian Runner

Khaki Campbell

HOUSING OPTIONS

Duck ark

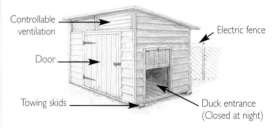

Air vent

Carrying handle

Nest

Duck entrance (closed at night)

↗ *Choose an ark that has been specifically designed for ducks – one that has sides that open for easy cleaning.*

Duck shed

Controllable ventilation

Electric fence

Door

Towing skids

Duck entrance (Closed at night)

↗ *Ideally, you need to choose a shed that is high enough for you to clean it out thoroughly without stooping.*

More options

Although duck houses now come in just about every shape and size that you can imagine, the traditional A-framed ark is still a great option, for the simple reason that it is easily portable. When the ground is stale and worn, you simply lift it and move it to a fresh patch. That said, some specialists favour a good-sized walk-around shed. The run needs to be ringed with a close-mesh chicken-wire fence (see page 44). If foxes are a pest, you have a choice of covering the whole run with a ceiling of mesh, or ringing the main fence with some sort of outer electric fence.

FEEDING

You need a special feeder, designed to keep the feed dry and off the ground, and a trough, bucket or pond for water. Apart from water and grit, the two primary feeding options are: (1) kitchen scraps, meal or layer's pellets, and a supply of fresh greens; (2) kitchen scraps, fresh greens, and traditional fare of potatoes, carrots and swedes.

WATER

The ideal is a pond that is wide and deep enough for the ducks to swim about and get their heads under the water; failing that, you could rig up one or more troughs plus some sort of fountain or shower.

The gravel slope gives the ducks easy access to and from the water.

Ducklings are best protected in a controlled area.

ROUTINE CARE

While most ducks can if necessary spend most of their lives out of doors, they generally do best if they are housed at night. If your ducks are overly noisy at night, the chances are that they are either too crowded, or not crowded enough. The ideal for a flock of 20 or so ducks is a house about 3 x 2.4 m (10 x 8 ft) – so that each duck has about 0.35 m (4 sq. ft) of floor space – enough to stretch and flap its wings. Ducks like a quiet life – not too much noise or fuss, a steady supply of food, a bit of shade to keep off the sun and rain, a dust bath, and water when they want it.

DUCKS FOR EATING

If the time comes when you want to kill a duck for eating, then make contact with a local duck society and ask for specialist hands-on advice.

TROUBLESHOOTING

TROUBLE	LIKELY CAUSES	POSSIBLE SOLUTIONS
One bird has a limp	Could be a any number of diseases, or a physical damage like a cut, splinter or tear	Wash and soak the foot in disinfectant and inspect it closely. Remove any foreign bodies and dress the wound with proprietary medication; visit a vet if the trouble continues
Messy eyes; the bird generally looks unhappy	Ducks need to be able to immerse their head in water; could be an eye infection or simply dry eyes	Wipe around the eyes with lukewarm soapy water to remove mess; make sure that the duck has access to enough water; check daily
The flock appears to be healthy, but shows loose and dirty plumage that generally looks to be in disarray	A messy, stale run, a dirty house, and a lack of dust and water	Clean the house and move it to a new run; supply a dust bath and a pond or trough
All the ducks are losing weight, with the feathers looking a bit scraggy, and the flesh looking inflamed	One of the external parasites such as red mites or lice, and/or a deficiency in the diet (some mites are so small that they are not easily visible with the naked eye)	Scrub and wash the house; powder the birds and the house with a proprietary medication; make sure that the diet is balanced
The whole flock looks ill at ease and the egg supply drops	Probably some sort of group fright or trauma such as low-flying aircraft, thunder and lightning, rats or a prowling fox	Make sure that the birds have plenty of water; calm the situation by increasing the feed; generally keep a watch for foxes and vermin

Keeping geese

Are geese worth considering?

If you have a patch of grass – something like an overgrown orchard – and plenty of kitchen scraps, geese can manage for most of the year without additional feeding. William Cobbett says in his classic book *Cottage Economy* (published in 1821) that 'geese are amongst the hardiest animals in the world ... a goose will lay a hundred eggs a year'. The profitable life of a goose is six times as long as that of a chicken.

CHOOSING A BREED

Look at your ground – the area, its character, the water supply, the amount of grass, fencing, shade and shelter, and then, bearing in mind that geese must have space to graze, work out what is possible.

- **Embden:** Good layer and good to eat; very hardy and relatively easy to keep. A healthy bird has glossy pure-white plumage and bright orange legs and feet. An average bird weighs about 8 kg (18 lb).
- **Roman:** Very popular breed, providing good eggs and good meat. Has a tall, upright carriage and pure-white plumage with orange-pink legs and feet. An average healthy bird weighs about 5.5–6.5 kg (12–14 lb).
- **Toulouse:** Can give up to 60 eggs a year, and is good to eat. Has grey, white-laced and mottled plumage, and orange legs and feet. A good bird weighs about 13.5 kg (30 lb).

Toulouse

Roman

Embden

HOUSING OPTIONS

Geese can be housed just about anywhere – a shed, a rough lean-to against the side of a barn, a temporary shelter made from straw bales topped with a tin roof – as long as it is fox-proof, high enough for the geese to stand up, dry, and with a box for them to lay eggs in. The immediate area around the shelter needs to be ringed with chicken wire (see page 44). You also need a feeder trough, and a trough or low bucket for water. As for foxes, while it is always best if the geese are locked in at night, a flock of half a dozen healthy geese will generally dissuade all but the most desperate fox. Geese can be quite aggressive, perhaps slightly dangerous and frightening for toddler-age children.

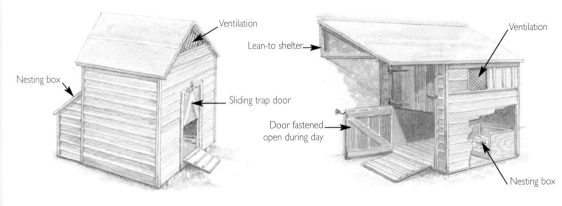

Ventilation

Nesting box

Sliding trap door

Lean-to shelter

Ventilation

Door fastened open during day

Nesting box

↗ *A basic goose house, with easy-access egg boxes, gable ventilation and a sliding drop door.*

↗ *A DIY goose house built against the side of an existing barn. The stable-type door allows for easy cleaning.*

FEEDING

Geese need grit, shell and a ready supply of water, and they will benefit from kitchen scraps and garden greens, but, those things apart, geese can derive most of their food by grazing. However, if you are trying to fatten them up or get them to produce lots of eggs, they will benefit from a feed of bran and oats, or pellets.

Geese make good guard 'dogs' – this pair will not allow strangers to approach the house.

ROUTINE CARE

While geese, unlike ducks or chickens, are happy to graze, they will take care of as much kitchen and garden waste as you can serve up. You could simply scatter their food and let the geese get on with it, but geese are so messy that it is advisable to feed them well away from the house. If you do take to feeding them, remember that, while geese are friendly and make good pets, they are large and can be aggressive. Apart from routinely cleaning their house, and making sure that there is always a ready supply of water, grit and shell, it is also a good idea to spend a few minutes every day checking the geese over – the way they stand, whether any are limping, whether the feathers look messy, or anything out of the ordinary that might point to a potential problem.

Geese need a water supply deep enough to immerse their heads.

GEESE FOR EATING

As with chickens and ducks, if the time comes when you want to kill a goose for the pot, then it is best to get advice from a member of a local poultry society.

TROUBLESHOOTING

TROUBLE	LIKELY CAUSES	POSSIBLE SOLUTIONS
Losing weight; one or more birds looking anaemic; lots of thin, splashy, watery droppings	If one bird is losing weight with the above symptoms, it could be something like an injury or poisoning; if more than one bird is losing weight, there are many disease possibilities	If you see a problem with a single bird, simply isolate the bird and see what happens; if the whole flock shows a problem, call in a vet
A sudden death	If an apparently healthy goose is found dead, the cause could be anything from trauma or leukaemia to pneumonia	Keep a close watch on the rest of the flock, in case there is a general problem, and call the vet if you see anything out of the ordinary
One or more birds have watery eyes; they are still on their feet, but generally looking miserable	Likely to be a cold	Isolate the bird(s) and make sure that the shed/hut/house is not wet or draughty; bathe the eyes and face with disinfectant, and keep watch; call the vet if the problem has not cleared up in about ten days
One or more birds are eating well but losing weight	Intestinal worms, picked up from contaminated ground	Dose with a proprietary medicine; clean the bird house, burn the bedding, and if possible move the birds to another site; isolate the bird(s) and see what happens

Keeping goats

What are the advantages of goats?

Goats are less expensive to buy than a cow, they are less choosy about food, and they produce very nutritious milk. However, while a cow will give 14–18 litres (3–4 gallons) a day, a goat will give only 3.5–4.5 litres (6–8 pints). Goats also see fences as a challenge, and they will eat almost anything – fruit trees, roses, all your vegetables, washing hanging on the line, children's toys, their shed – but they still fit nicely into a self-sufficiency scheme.

CHOOSING A BREED

Take a long look at your set-up – the amount of land, the state of the fences, the water, your primary needs – and consider how keeping a goat will be a big commitment in terms of time. Weekdays, weekends, holidays, wet, windy and sunny days – you or a helper will have to be on hand at all times. Finally, having carefully thought through all the implications and decided to go ahead, make contact with a goat society.

- **Alpine:** Very popular large breed, jet black with white markings; gives quality milk, but is restless and needs plenty of space.

- **Anglo Nubian:** Large animal, red tan through to black and white in colour; good choice if you are looking for a high milk yield with a high butter-fat content.
- **Angora:** Good milkers, and good-natured, but really bred for their mohair (quality mohair can fetch a high price).
- **Saanen:** Good all-rounder, with a short, fine coat; good option if you want to milk throughout the winter.
- **Toggenburg:** Very popular breed, much favoured by beginners who are looking to get a good milk yield at a relatively low feed cost; the silky tan-brown to white coloured coat is much favoured by spinners.

Angora   *Saanen*   *Toggenburg*

HOUSING OPTIONS

Ideally, the goat house needs to be well built, weathertight and roomy enough for you and the goats to move around in. Four goats need a shed about 2.4 m (8 ft) wide and 4.8 m (16 ft) long – so that each goat has a stall about 2.4 m (8 ft) long and 1.2 m (4 ft) wide. When planning your particular set-up, imagine yourself dealing with the goats, and then build the house accordingly. You want to move around the goat house without stooping, there must be a tap for water, a cupboard, a milking area, a place for washing your hands and doing the milking, and so on. The compound needs a wire-mesh fence about 1.2–1.5 m (4–5 ft) high, and the field needs an electric wire-strand fence.

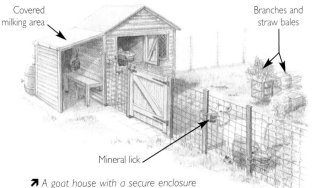

Covered milking area

Branches and straw bales

Mineral lick

↗ *A goat house with a secure enclosure and an integral milking house.*

These Nigerian dairy goats, owned by the Caldwell family in Oregon, USA, like nothing better than searching out their own food.

FEEDING

- Goats kept indoors must have an unlimited supply of water and hay, a salt lick, and a daily feed of oats and maize, or concentrated goat feed.
- Goats kept outdoors need a piece of scrubland for browsing, plus about 5.5 kg (12 lb) of hay every day in cold weather.
- Goats in milk must have a supplement of oats and hay, or a special feed.

BREEDING

- The female goat is ready for mating when she is about 18 months old.
- She will be ready in the autumn, when the vulva shows wet and red and the tail wags from side to side.
- She will have a three-day-long season every 21 days until she is mated.
- The easiest option for mating is to take your goat to stud.
- The gestation period averages about 150 days. When she is due, her udder will start to grow and fill, the vulva will show a discharge, and she will become unsettled and noisy.
- It is advisable for the first birth to call in qualified help.

MILKING

Leave the mother with the kid(s) for about two weeks and then take them off and start milking. Some goat-keepers milk twice a day, others just once. The once-a-day option gives less milk. When you are ready to milk, put the goat on a leash and lead her to the clean area that you have set aside for milking. Put her on a platform so that she is at a comfortable working height, clip the leash to the wall, fit a hobble on her back legs, and wash the udder with warm water. To milk,

encircle a single teat with thumb and hand, gently squeeze with the thumb so that the milk in the lower part of the teat is under pressure, and apply a gentle downward stroking movement so that the milk squirts out. Clean the teat hole by wasting the first squirt, and then direct the milk into your pail or bowl. Do one teat and then the other.

MILKING QUESTIONS AND ANSWERS

- **How do I treat the fresh milk?** Take the milk indoors and strain it through several layers of clean white-cotton cloth or filter paper, and store it in the fridge ready for use.
- **Can I freeze the milk?** Yes. Pour the milk into freezer bags and stack them in the freezer.
- **What does goat's milk taste like?** It tastes creamy with a nutty background flavour.
- **Can I miss a day's milking?** Yes, if the kids are at hand to drink her dry. Some milkers advocate milking once a day.
- **How long will the mother stay in milk?** Most milkers aim for about 6–7 months of milking, followed by four months of rest.
- **Will the doe give milk without having kids?** No, she must have babies.

Secure the goat that is to be milked on a platform so that she is at a comfortable working height for you.

Keeping sheep

Are sheep easy to look after?

Sheep are docile and relatively easy to handle. They will fatten on middling to poor grass, and will give both meat and wool. A six-ewe flock could be very rewarding, in fact a good skill-stretching challenge, for a keen beginner. On the other hand, not only will you have to be prepared to deal with all the maladies, parasites, bugs, sickness and infections that readily attack sheep, but you will also have to learn the gentle art of sheep shearing.

CHOOSING A BREED

Once you have decided to keep sheep, you must look at your set-up – the size and character of your land – and assess your aims. Do you want meat for home use or for market? Do you want wool? Or do you want both? Are you going to adopt the traditional spring-summer-autumn-winter system that involves lambing in spring, fattening in summer, and killing in autumn? Or are you planning to keep rare breeds for their fleeces rather than their meat?

There are three main classes of sheep: 'long-woolled', including Devon Long-wool, Leicestershire, Border Leicestershire, Wensleydale, Cotswolds, Hampshire Down and Lincoln; 'short-woolled', including South Down, Suffolk and Dorset; and 'mountain sheep', including Jacob, Welsh Mountain, Cheviot, Dartmoor and Black-faced.

- **Border Leicester:** Big and strong with a white or black face and coarse fleece; good for meat.
- **Jacob:** Lean, strong, multicoloured, with good-looking horns, grown primarily for their wool; the fleece is good for spinning and weaving, and much favoured by spinners for its texture and multicolours.
- **Merino:** Reared primarily for the fine-textured wool, which is generally considered to be of the best quality.
- **Southdown:** Strong and compact with a dense, tight fleece; good for eating and for wool.
- **Suffolk:** Large, strong, compact and white- or black-faced, with a tight, curly coat that produces top-quality, fine-fibred wool; good for lowlands; good to eat.

Sheep like trees because they provide the perfect place to shelter from wind and rain, and are also good to rub against.

Jacob

Suffolk

Border Leicester

HOUSING OPTIONS

Fencing stakes

Roof tied down

Straw bales

↗ *At lambing time, build a temporary shelter close to the house so that you don't have to walk too far in wind and rain.*

Apart from a rough shelter at lambing time, sheep live most of their lives out of doors. A good low-cost option is to build a temporary shelter – from square bales of straw, corrugated iron, poles and rope – close to your home, so that the sheep are conveniently nearby at lambing time.

FEEDING

- Most sheep are 'grass sheep', meaning that they can thrive on average to poor pasture.
- Just before and after lambing, the ewes will need extra food – corn, chopped swedes or concentrated pellets.
- To fatten lambs up, you need to feed them swedes, hay and linseed cake.
- In winter, feed the remaining ewes with hay, plus a rising intake of supplements as winter runs into spring and on into lambing time.

Lambs can be bottle-fed like a baby, and then later trained to suckle from a mechanical 'mum'.

BREEDING

- Sheep are sexually mature in their second year.
- Ewes mated in autumn will produce lambs about 21 weeks later, in the spring of the following year.
- When a ewe is ready to lamb, she will lie down and start groaning and straining.
- The water bag appears first, followed by the lamb's nose and two feet, and finally the head and shoulders.
- Once the lamb is out, the mother will start licking all the mess away from the lamb's face.
- The lamb will – must – suckle within a couple of hours of being born.
- Lambs can be bottle-fed with formula milk, just like a baby.
- If you are a raw beginner, you will most definitely need help and advice. Make contact with a vet and/or an experienced farmer well before the birthing date.

Warning

Some sheep diseases can cross over to humans – especially to pregnant women and young children – so avoid close contact with the bodily fluids of the ewes or lambs.

SHEARING

The best way of learning to shear – some would say the only way – is to watch an expert. All you need is a complete set of old clothes, a pair of hand shears, a friend to help hold and catch the sheep, a nice clean area of deep grass, and lots of patience. Upend and straddle the sheep, ease the wool to be cut with one hand, and gently cut it away with the shears held in the other. The easiest course of action is to sit the sheep on its lower back, trim around the head and neck, and then work down the belly and out and round towards the back. Don't try to rush the task, just take your time, and be careful not to nip the skin. Most of the trick is in holding the sheep – if you get that right the rest will follow.

However, if you choose a time when the weather is very hot, you will find that the fleece can be rolled or plucked, more or less uncut, from the sheep's body. In the Shetland Isles, this procedure is termed 'rooing', meaning plucking.

SHEEP FOR EATING

A healthy lamb is a beautiful animal, but normally the harsh reality is that you are keeping sheep for the lambs – for their meat. When the time comes for slaughter, make contact with your vet and a registered abattoir, and let them guide you through the various procedures.

Keeping a cow

How easy you will find keeping and milking a cow depends on your set-up, the time and effort you are prepared to put in, and the character of the cow. Some cows enjoy being milked; others hate it. Cows like routine, plenty of food, warm hands and calm; they dislike loud noises, sudden movements and a grabbing milking action. If you get it right, keeping a cow will be most rewarding. Talk to experts and thoroughly research before you consider keeping a cow.

A Shetland – small, black and white – makes a wonderful house cow. They are hardy, have a good temperament and are easy to milk.

CHOOSING A BREED

Although in many ways the easiest option for beginners is to get a cow who is on her second calf, meaning a cow who has already been hand-milked, the disadvantage of this option is that you will immediately be presented with the challenge of looking after a cow and her calf. If you go for this scenario you will have to be well prepared and organized. The following list describes some common breeds.

- **Dexter:** Small; black or red coat; becoming rare; good to milk; high-yielding.
- **Friesian:** Large; black and white coat; has a very high milk yield.
- **Jersey:** Medium-sized; light brown coat; makes a good house cow; medium yield of rich cream and milk; good temperament; easy to handle; needs housing in winter.

Dexter   Friesian   Jersey

BREEDING

- Cows are ready to be put to the bull, or artificially inseminated, when they are about 24 months old; the precise time depends on the breed.
- The easiest option for getting a cow in calf is to send her to a bull.
- A cow can only be mated when she is in heat, usually indicated by a mucus discharge and skittish behaviour.
- The gestation period, the time from mating to calving, is about nine months.
- The easiest plan for the timing is to have your cow mated in summer so she calves in spring.
- From about seven months into the pregnancy you have to increase the cow's feed – oats, hay and a nice mix of whatever food is available.
- When the cow's time is near, her udders will fill and her back end will go loose and slack.
- If all goes well, the calf will be presented in much the same way as a sheep or goat – the water bag will appear, followed closely by a nose and two feet, and then the head and shoulders.
- Once the calf is out, the mother will lick it into action.
- The ideal is for the cow to give birth unaided – you should not have to lend a hand.
- Read the books, talk to local farmers, and have telephone numbers at the ready, but the best advice is to have a vet or an experienced farmer close at hand to provide help and guidance.

WEANING

When it comes to weaning the calf away from the mother, choose one of the following options to suit your set-up.

- You can let the calf have all the milk for week and then gradually take it away and teach it to feed from a bottle or bucket.
- You can milk the cow and give the calf a mix of water and milk.
- You and the calf can have a pair of teats each for the first month or so.
- You can let the calf feed for a limited number of hours per day, and then top him/her up with a milk supplement.

Teach the calf to feed from a teat or bucket.

You will soon get the hang of gently hand milking your cow.

QUESTIONS AND ANSWERS

- **Is hand milking difficult?** Technically, hand milking is easy; you just take hold of the teat in one hand, exert pressure with your thumb and index finger, and gently squeeze with a rolling action of your fingers.
- **How much hay does a cow need?** One cow needs about one tonne of hay for winter feed.
- **How much land do I need?** A good option is to have about 1 hectare (about 2 acres) – half for the cow, and half for making the tonne of hay. You could manage with half this amount if you are you going to buy in the hay.
- **What can I do with the excess milk?** You could feed it to the calf or calves to fatten them up, you could make butter and cheese, or you could give it to other livestock such as pigs or chickens.
- **Do I have to milk twice a day?** Yes you will have to milk twice a day (TAD) if you want maximum yield, but if you are happy with less milk you can get away with milking once a day (OAD).
- **Do I have to milk every day?** Yes, if the cow is in milk, you (or a helper) have to milk at least once every single day of the year.
- **Is butter-making as difficult as it sounds?** It is not difficult so much as time-consuming.

Once the cows are out in the meadow – secure and away from traffic noise and dogs – they can be left to get on with it.

Keeping pigs

What are 'weaners'?

To start, you could search around for a couple of orphaned piglets, or buy a couple of 8–9-week-old weaners – pigs that have just been weaned. The weaners will be more expensive, but they will be healthier and less of a gamble. Two pigs will be happier, and easier to fatten, than a single pig. They are ideal for clearing an old orchard or an overgrown kitchen garden prior to new planting. A pair of growing pigs will dig and manure a vegetable plot without being asked!

QUESTIONS AND ANSWERS

- **Should I start by breeding pigs?** The easiest option if you are a beginner is to fatten a couple of weaners with excess milk, and kitchen and garden scraps. Later, when you have learned something about the character and behaviour of pigs, and when you have a clearer understanding of your skills and needs, you can try breeding.
- **Why get two pigs?** Pigs are social animals – they enjoy company. A single pig will be a lonely animal. Two pigs will sleep, play and frolic together, and a pair of happy pigs will fatten up nicely.
- **Can I keep pigs indoors in my barn?** Lots of people do keep pigs indoors in barns, sheds and purpose-made pig sties, but it is much more fun for you and the pigs if you keep them outdoors. Pigs are happiest when they are rooting about in the soil, playing together, digging wallows, getting muddy and generally being a pig.
- **What type of fence do I need?** The easiest and most efficient option is to make good your existing fence, hedge, wall or other barrier, and set up a modern electric fence just inside the boundary.
- **Can I keep pigs in my overgrown orchard?** An overgrown orchard would be the perfect place for pigs – they will clear the weeds, dig up grubs and pests, eat windfalls, and generally bring the orchard to order.

- **Can I give my pigs leftover meat pies from the local café?** Although it is true that pigs will eat just about anything, and although they have traditionally been fed on swill from restaurants, you should not let them eat meat. Bread, fruit pies, fruit and vegetables, chips – but not meat.

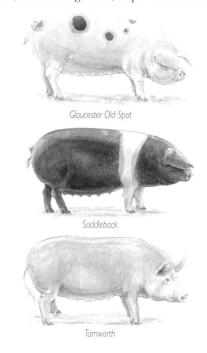

Gloucester Old Spot

Saddleback

Tamworth

CHOOSING A BREED

The easiest option is to go for one of the older rarer breeds – they are hardier, tougher and generally better able to take care of themselves.
- **Gloucester Old Spot:** One of the less common breeds; can be white with black spots or vice versa; hardy, docile and generally good-natured; good for outdoors.
- **Large Black:** Large, black-haired, traditional lop-eared pig; good temperament; ideal for keeping outdoors.
- **Saddleback:** There are two saddleback breeds – Essex Saddleback and Wessex Saddleback; both are black with a white band; hardy, so very good for outdoors.
- **Tamworth:** Good-sized; sandy or reddish in colour; long snout; good for outdoors.

A happy top-quality Saddleback pig, with good housing, good feeding, and plenty of space to roam around in.

HOUSING OPTIONS

A pig house can be just about anything from an A-frame hut knocked together from timber and corrugated iron, or a specially built sty made from brick and tiles, to a temporary shelter made from hay bales topped with sheets of corrugated iron. Anything will do, as long as it is strong, low to the ground and built so that it will keep off the sun, wind and rain.

↗ *A temporary shelter of hay bales and sheets of corrugated iron makes a good house.*

FEEDING

- Pigs enjoy and thrive on routine. They must be fed at regular intervals – 2–3 times a day.
- Traditionally, pig breeders reckon to give a pig as much food as it can eat in 20 minutes.
- Pigs must have water on demand – at least 1 litre (2 pints) of water for every 450 g (1 lb) of feed.
- Weaners need three good feeds every day, plus all they can find.
- When the pigs are out on good grass, you can balance the supplementary feeds with the grass – good grass with low feed, poor grass with good feed.
- Feed basic meals for the first 16 weeks, and then feed to fatten.
- Pigs do very well on wild food such as acorns, sweet chestnuts, beechnuts and elderberries.

PIGS FOR EATING

If you would like to kill a pig for eating, make contact with a local pig society or slaughterhouse for advice.

TROUBLESHOOTING

TROUBLE	LIKELY CAUSES	POSSIBLE SOLUTIONS
Rapid breathing, restlessness, vomiting	Could be something as simple as heat exhaustion, but could also be something serious such as foot and mouth	If the pig has obviously been in the sun and overheated, spray with water and give a saline drench – meaning a forced drink; if there is no apparent cause, send for the vet
Pig not eating, staying in bed, breathing heavily, and generally looking unwell	Could be pneumonia	If the sty is wet, cold and draughty, the pig should be moved to a warmer house; colds and chills are more likely to affect indoor pigs that are put out rather than outdoor pigs that are used to hardier conditions
The pig is a huge greedy eater and yet does not put on any weight	Probably one of the 40–50 types of worms that trouble pigs	Ask the vet for a worm treatment, dose regularly, and move the pig to a new piece of ground
Loss of appetite, listlessness and no dung	Constipation, no bowel movement; some sort of obstruction in the bowel	Ask the vet for a purgative, make the feed sloppier, give clean bedding, and provide a bit of heat if the weather is cold
Pig dies suddenly	If the cause is clear to see (say a cut leg and subsequent bleeding), the cause is obvious; otherwise there could be any number of causes	If the death is sudden and there is no obvious physical injury, contact the vet and ask for a post-mortem; in some countries you are required by law to notify the police
Pigs fighting with each other	This can be a problem if you bring in a new lone pig, or a pig that is obviously smaller; older pigs and sows will also fight	Make sure there is enough room for every pig to claim its bit of space; traditionally, pig-keepers used to spray aniseed oil over all the pigs – new and old – so that all the pigs had the same smell

Keeping bees

*Can I keep
bees in a
small garden?*

Generally, keeping bees in any garden is fine, as long as you follow a few ground rules. Make sure the hives are placed so that the flight path is well away from neighbouring fences. Also build a plastic-mesh screen, 2.4 m (8 ft) high, around the hives so that the bees are forced to rise well into the air before leaving the garden. Your neighbours must be happy with the arrangement – if they are not, then you will have to think again.

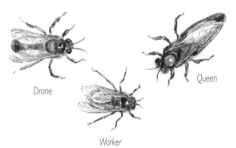

Drone

Queen

Worker

QUESTIONS AND ANSWERS

- **What if I am allergic to bee stings?** Sooner or later, you will get stung, so you must start out by having an allergy test – just in case you are hypersensitive.
- **Can I make money by selling honey?** Although I have said in the past that beekeeping will, if you are averagely lucky, pay for itself, keep you in honey and maybe bring in a little money, currently there is a lot of interest in honey – so much so that some keen beekeepers are doing very well selling their honey. So, yes, maybe you can make money.
- **Where can I get hands-on advice?** Read all the available literature and make contact with a local beekeeping association. Tell them that you are looking for advice, and explain that you want to know about set-up stock and so on. You will be able to pal up with a beekeeper and learn by helping and watching him or her at work.
- **What type of honey can I expect?** Bees will collect nectar from a 3 km (2 mile) radius of their hive, so a couple of days spent walking, observing and taking notes will tell you what sort of honey you can expect – clover, rape, lavender, for example. The local bee society will also have all the answers.
- **Is beekeeping time-consuming?** It depends upon your goal. You could either spend two long days every year tending the hives, with lots of swift passing inspections in between, or inspect your hives thoroughly every two weeks from mid-spring until late summer.
- **How many hives are best?** One hive is a bad idea – it is a bit too much like putting all your eggs in one basket. Two hives are better, but three are perfect. You will find it to be a skill-stretching challenge, you will be able to compare the performance of one hive against another, and bees also perform best when they are in the company of other bees – they are happy when they are in communities.

THE HIVE

The ideal site

The ideal site is a safe, private, secure and sheltered spot within about 3 km (2 miles) of an orchard, heather-clad hills, fields of flowering crops such as clover and rape, or decorative gardens – anywhere where the bees can gather pollen. The hives are best arranged so that they are sheltered from cold winds and squally rain, and warmed by early-morning sunshine.

A 'National' hive

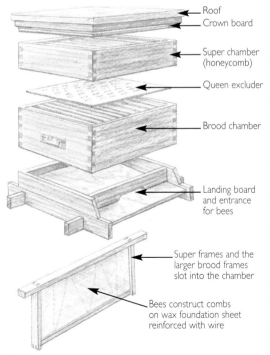

Roof
Crown board

Super chamber
(honeycomb)

Queen excluder

Brood chamber

Landing board
and entrance
for bees

Super frames and the
larger brood frames
slot into the chamber

Bees construct combs
on wax foundation sheet
reinforced with wire

↗ *A National Langstroth hive – made to an international standard size – is the easiest option.*

Beekeeping glossary

- **Apiary** Group of hives.

- **Base** The base on which the hive sits; this might be anything from a wooden frame with legs through to a stack of concrete blocks.

- **Bee-driving** Term used to describe the process of transferring bees from a skep (straw beehive) or box to a new hive.

- **Bee-escape** Small arrangement fitted within the hive that allows the bees to move down but not to return.

- **Bee space** A 6–9 mm (¼–⅜ in) space between component parts of the hive.

- **Bee suit** Complete coverall outfit designed to protect you from the bees, made up of a boiler suit with a hat, veil and gloves, with elastic at the ankles, wrists and neck.

- **Bottom board** The floor of a beehive, a gently sloping board that runs from the back of the hive through to the front.

- **Brace comb** Component part that links two combs.

- **Brood chambers** Middle part of the hive in which the brood is reared.

- **Cell** Hexagonal part of a honeycomb.

- **Comb foundation** Man-made structure made up of thin sheets of beeswax and stamped with a cell pattern.

- **Feeding** The procedure of giving the bees a feed of sugar or syrup.

- **Frame** Four pieces of wood designed to hold a honeycomb, like a small picture frame.

- **Hive body** The total wooden structure that holds and encloses the frames.

- **Hives** There are two basic hives – the traditional double-walled hive (now hardly used) and the 'National' or 'Commercial' hive (see 'Langstroth equipment').

- **Langstroth equipment** Term used to describe modern, standard-sized hives, named after the Reverend L.L. Langstroth who published a book on beekeeping in the mid-nineteenth century.

- **Queen excluder** Device in the form of a pierced sheet of wood or metal that restricts the drones and queens to set parts of the hive.

- **Robing** When one hive of bees steals the syrups, sugar or honey from another hive.

- **Smoker** Device with bellows and nozzle that puffs smoke, used to subdue bees, sometimes also called a 'bellows smoker'.

- **Super** Any part of the hive used for storing honey; one of the layers or chambers.

A fully protected beekeeper at work. Note the outfit, the smoker and the location of the hives.

TRADITIONAL HIVES

These might be any shape, size or structure, and made out of any material – with shapes relating to periods, countries and districts. They look pretty, but they cannot be used with modern, standardized Langstroth equipment.

PESTS

Bees can be bothered by mice, ants, insect-eating birds, other insects, wasps and parasites. The best you can do is use physical methods of keeping the pests at bay – traps and barriers for the mice, the legs of the hive sitting in bowls of paraffin for the ants, and windmill scarers for the birds.

EXTRACTING HONEY

Traditionally, the honey was separated by crushing the comb and sieving off the honey – a procedure that involved destroying the comb. The modern practice involves removing the combs complete with their frames, slicing the caps off the cells with a long straight-sided knife, placing the uncapped combs in an extracting machine – a machine that looks a bit like a salad dryer or a spin-dryer – and winding a handle so that the honey is spun by centrifugal force out of the combs and into the outer vat. Once in the outer vat of the container, the honey is drawn off through a little tap.

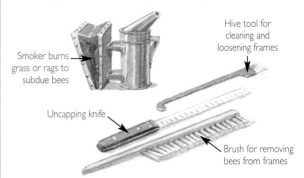

Smoker burns grass or rags to subdue bees

Hive tool for cleaning and loosening frames

Uncapping knife

Brush for removing bees from frames

You don't need much equipment, so it pays to get the best.

Storing food

How can I store any surplus?

There are many good methods of preserving food, including salting, drying, smoking, bottling, potting, and making jams, chutneys and pickles. To store foods whole, you can bury root vegetables under straw and earth, you can place fruits such as apples in a dry, dark, well-aired cupboard, and you can pickle eggs. Also, if you want to go for an expensive, less 'eco' option, you can freeze just about everything.

HEALTH ISSUES

While you can salt, smoke and dry both fish and meat, the fact is that fish and meat are responsible for more food-poisoning than any other foods. However, most of these outbreaks have occurred with shellfish, chicken and pork eaten in restaurants. However, the easiest and safest option if you are concerned about problems associated with, for example, smoking meat and fish, is in the first instance to concentrate your efforts on smoking cheese, and then think about meat and fish when you have perfected your smoking techniques.

POPULAR STORE ITEMS

- **Jam:** It is easy to make (see pages 62–63) and the results are excellent.

- **Dried mushrooms:** Drying mushrooms is a fool-proof procedure, direct and low-cost.

- **Cheese and butter:** A tried and trusted way of using excess milk.

- **Chutney:** It is easy to make and can be eaten with bread and cheese, salads or curries.

- **Pickles:** Vegetables such as small onions or beetroot, nuts and garlic can be pickled in vinegar.

- **Apples:** To store, wrap in newspaper and place in the dark.

- **Eggs:** They will keep for 2–3 months if they are taken straight from the hen, wrapped in newspaper and stored in a cool, dark place.

- **Salted runner beans:** Layer fresh sliced runner beans and salt in a jar.

- **Bottled apple pulp:** Peel and slice the apples, boil them to a thick pulp and bottle.

Storing root vegetables

Root crops like potatoes, carrots, turnips and beet are best stored in a clamp. The procedure for clamping up potatoes is to select a well-drained corner of the garden, heap the potatoes on a bed of dry straw on a layer of sand, cover the heap with more straw, and then bury it all under 20 cm (8 in) or so of dry earth.

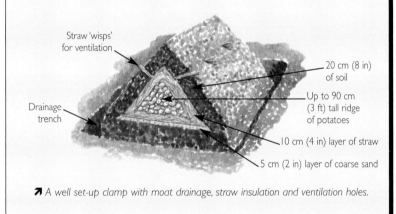

Straw 'wisps' for ventilation

Drainage trench

20 cm (8 in) of soil

Up to 90 cm (3 ft) tall ridge of potatoes

10 cm (4 in) layer of straw

5 cm (2 in) layer of coarse sand

↗ A well set-up clamp with moat drainage, straw insulation and ventilation holes.

Storing apples

Crisp apples can be stored as they are. Carefully hand-pick choice apples one at a time, check that they are completely free from holes, wrap them in crisp, dry newspaper, and then layer them in a cardboard box, line them up on a shelf, or stack in wooden boxes. The apples must be stored in a cool, dry, dark, frost-free place.

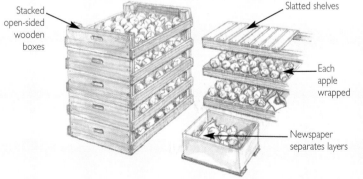

Stacked open-sided wooden boxes

Slatted shelves

Each apple wrapped

Newspaper separates layers

↗ Apples are best stored in stacking wooden boxes so there is plenty of ventilation.

Storing cabbages

Dense white cabbages can be stored simply by picking them fresh. Cut off any damaged leaves, and hang them in nets in a cool, dry, dark, frost-free shed.

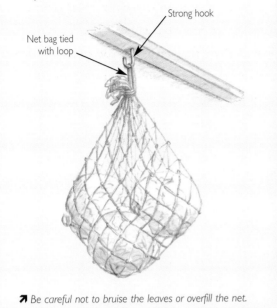

Strong hook

Net bag tied with loop

↗ *Be careful not to bruise the leaves or overfill the net.*

Storing onions

Onions can be dried and hung up in a cool, dark, dry, well-ventilated shed. Take two lengths of string, knot them together to make a double string, tie a weight at one end, and hang it from the ceiling so that the strings are side by side and taut. Take the well-dried onions one at a time, and, starting from the bottom, thread the dried stalks through the paired strings.

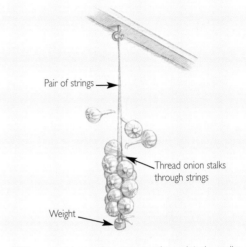

Pair of strings

Thread onion stalks through strings

Weight

↗ *Some people use three strings; others plait the stalks.*

Storing herbs

The easiest way of storing most herbs is to dry them. Take a bunch of herbs, put the head of the bunch in a brown-paper bag, loosely tie the bag in place, and hang the herbs, bag and all, up in a warm, dry place. When the herbs are crisp-dry, scrunch them up so that the dried leaves are held and contained in the bag. See also page 67 for tips on drying herbs.

Bamboo cane

↗ *Use paper bags (not plastic), so the herbs stay dry.*

Storing pumpkins and marrows

Pumpkins and marrows are easily stored. Pick the pumpkins or marrows when they are dry, inspect them to make sure they are in perfect condition, place them carefully in nets, and hang them in a cool, dry, dark, frost-free place.

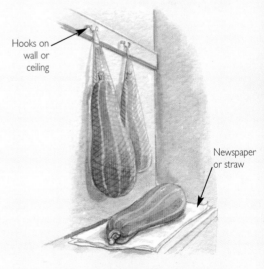

Hooks on wall or ceiling

Newspaper or straw

↗ *Check regularly to make sure they are still firm.*

Making jam

If you find that you have a surplus of fruit, a good way of preserving it is to make jam. There will be some expense for the pan, heat and sugar, but the cost and effort are nothing compared to the pleasure of looking at all the jars lined up on the shelf, the enjoyment of giving it away to friends, and the simple delight of eating amazingly tasty home-made jam. Be warned: once the kids and friends and family get to taste your home-made jam you will have a job for life.

For top-quality jam, it pays to pick the fruit when it is ripe and firm.

INGREDIENTS

Traditional jam is made from three ingredients: fresh fruit, good-quality sugar and water. The fruit is gently cooked with water until the natural pectins and acids have been extracted; sugar is added, and then the mixture is simmered until the magical moment when the liquid suddenly thickens and turns to jam. When this stage is reached, the jam is ladled into jars, the jars are capped with airtight lids and the jam is allowed to cool. A good jam will be firm in consistency, brilliant in colour, evenly textured, and true to the flavour of the fruit. The jars will be filled to the brim, the lids will be tight, and the contents will last without losing their flavour. If you have only ever tasted shop-bought jam, rest assured that home-made jam is something totally different.

BASIC JAM-MAKING EQUIPMENT

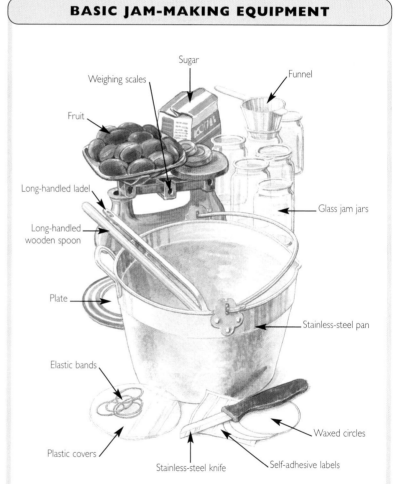

Sugar

Weighing scales

Funnel

Fruit

Long-handled ladle

Glass jam jars

Long-handled wooden spoon

Plate

Stainless-steel pan

Elastic bands

Plastic covers

Stainless-steel knife

Waxed circles

Self-adhesive labels

The jam-making kit illustrated above is based on the simple premise that nothing goes in the jam apart from fresh fruit, water and sugar, and that you are going to boil the fruit and water in the pan, add sugar, stir the mixture with a long-handled wooden spoon or paddle, use a long-handled ladle or a jug to pour the mixture by way of a funnel into jars, cap the jars with plastic covers, and generally be working in a kitchen that is averagely equipped with plates, boards, cloths and so on.

BASIC JAM-MAKING METHOD

1 Select and prepare the fresh fruit – the amount according to the recipe – and wash and generally remove cores, pips, peel and stalks, as appropriate. Discard decayed or squashy fruit. Weigh the prepared fruit.

2 Smear the inside of the pan with butter or margarine to reduce the formation of sugar scum.

3 Weigh the prepared fruit and slide it into the pan along with the appropriate quantity of water.

4 Turn on the heat, bring to the boil and simmer until the fruit has broken down.

5 Sterilize the jam jars by heating them in the oven at 150°C (300°F)/gas mark 2 for 15 minutes.

6 Add the sugar little by little, stirring all the time. Continue simmering and stirring until the mixture gently bubbles even when it is stirred.

7 To test it, spoon a puddle of jam onto a cold plate, allow to cool for half a minute, and then push it with your fingernail. If the little puddle of jam wrinkles, it is ready to pot.

8 When the jam is ready, turn off the heat, take the jars (all washed clean, dried and warmed), put them on a wooden surface and use the funnel and a ladle, jug or mug to fill them up with jam.

9 As soon as each jar is filled, place the waxed circle, wax side down, on the jam and fit the cover. Label and date the jars, and store them in a cool, dark, dry, frost-free cupboard.

Covering

SPECIAL TIPS

• **Health and safety:** Hot jam is extremely dangerous. You must be careful at every stage not to burn your hands. Wear a good coverall apron, and shoes rather than sandals or slippers. Make sure children stay well clear of the boiling jam; help avoid accidents by warning them of the dangers and keeping equipment out of reach.

• **Covers and seals:** Without covers and seals the jam would go bad. Most people use jam-cover kits that consist of transparent discs of cellophane or some other plastic, discs of waxed paper, and elastic bands. You push the waxed circles down onto the hot jam, dampen the plastic discs and spread them over the jar tops, and secure them with the elastic bands. A well-fitting cover will be stretched to creating a drum-tight surface.

• **Pectin:** The presence of pectin is vital – without it the jam will not set. Because firm, ripe fruit is high in pectin, while over-ripe, squashy fruit is low, it is most important that you choose the former. If you think that the fruit is low in pectin – either because the recipe suggests that the fruit you are using is naturally low in pectin, or you have no choice other than to use fruit that is overly ripe – you can increase the pectin by adding lemons.

• **How much water?** Too much water and the fruit will not soften and release its pectin, and may burn; too much water and the jam will not thicken and set. If you have to make a mistake, then too much water is better than too little, since you can make good by cooking to evaporate the excess water.

JAM RECIPES

Apple and blackberry jam
This traditional recipe is a good way of making the most of a glut of apples. If you dislike the blackberry pips, cook the blackberries separately and run them through a sieve before adding to the apples.

Ingredients:
• 450 g (1 lb) cooking apples (Bramleys are best)
• 1.4 kg (3 lb) blackberries
• 285 ml (½ pint) water
• 1.8 kg (4 lb) sugar

Method:
1 Peel, core and slice the apples, dropping them in a bowl of water as you go to keep their colour. Drain and weigh them after preparation.
2 Wash the blackberries and remove the stalks, and weigh them after preparation.
3 Put all the fruit in the pan with the water and simmer until the fruit is soft.
4 Add the sugar and simmer until the jam is set.

Apple and damson jam
A very good, strong-flavoured, traditional country jam if you have a mixed orchard. If you want to use plums rather than damsons, either use purple or dark blue plums, or use Victoria plums and add lemons.

Ingredients:
• 900 g (2 lb) cooking apples (Bramleys are best)
• 900 g (2 lb) damsons
• 570 ml (1 pint) water
• 1.8 kg (4 lb) sugar

Method:
1 Peel, core and slice the apples, dropping them in a bowl of water as you go to keep their colour. Drain and weigh them after preparation.
2 Wash and stone the damsons and weigh them after preparation.
3 Put all the fruit in the pan with the water and simmer until the fruit is soft.
4 Add the sugar and simmer until the jam is set.

Alan's Seville orange marmalade
This is a lazy man's twist on a traditional recipe – the colour is a bit dull, but it has a strong taste, it is fast and the end result has so much character that it can be spooned onto roast duck or into a curry. If you like smooth marmalade, but still want to get the job done fast, chop the fruit until you like the texture.

Ingredients:
• 900 g (2 lb) Seville oranges
• 2 large lemons
• 2.2 litres (4 pints) water
• 1.8 kg (4 lb) sugar

Method:
1 Wash the oranges thoroughly and cut off and discard the top-and-tail ends.
2 Quarter the oranges and remove pips. Weigh the prepared fruit.
3 Do the same with the lemons.
4 Put the oranges and lemons in a kitchen processor and swiftly chop them to a rough mess.
5 Put all the fruit in the pan with the water and simmer until the fruit is soft.
6 Add the sugar and simmer until the marmalade is set.

Making chutney

Chutney-making is a swift, easy and low-cost way of preserving vegetables and fruit that would otherwise be difficult to save. For example, you might have a glut of onions and cooking apples. You could pickle the onions in vinegar and dry or bottle the apples, but chutney made from a mixture of onions and apples is simple to do and makes a delicious accompaniment to many different foods. As for taste, home-made chutney is perfect with bread and cheese.

The basic mix of ingredients can be modified to suit your taste.

ADAPTING RECIPES TO SUIT YOUR TASTE

Chutney is a winner on many counts. It is wonderfully easy to make – you just gather your chosen fruit, vegetables, sugar, spices and vinegar, put them in a pan, bring the mixture to the boil, simmer until it thickens, and that is about it. The whole business of making chutney allows you to be creative, however. If you do not like a certain ingredient, or you have a surplus of something, you can modify the recipe to suit. For example, if you are faced with a traditional onion, tomato and apple recipe, and you do not like one of the ingredients – say sultanas – but are very keen on the onions, and your partner loves apples, you can simply drop the sultanas and increase the apples and onions. Chutney-making is very forgiving: if it is too thin, you can add more sugar and simmer and reduce; if it is too thick, you can add more vinegar.

BASIC CHUTNEY-MAKING EQUIPMENT

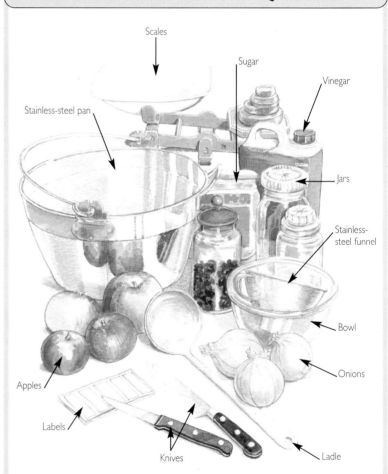

Scales

Sugar

Vinegar

Stainless-steel pan

Jars

Stainless-steel funnel

Bowl

Onions

Apples

Labels

Knives

Ladle

Apart from all the usual tools and pieces of equipment that you might expect to find in the average kitchen, you need a good-sized pair of scales, a large stainless-steel pan, a jug, mug or ladle, a stainless-steel or plastic funnel, and lots of jars complete with lids or caps. The whole chutney-making procedure is that much easier if you have lots of space, plenty of work surfaces, and unlimited plates and bowls.

BASIC CHUTNEY-MAKING METHOD

Filling jars

1 Select and prepare all the ingredients: wash, peel and core apples, peel onions, remove plum pips, and generally make sure the ingredients are clean and free from stalks, pips, cores and so on.

2 Chop or mince the ingredients, finely or coarsely according to taste.

3 Put the chopped ingredients into the pan with spices according to the recipe.

4 Cover with vinegar.

5 Turn on the heat and gently simmer for 1–4 hours until the contents are soft.

6 Dissolve the sugar in some part of the vinegar and add to the mixture.

7 Wash and dry the jars and put them in the oven. Bring the oven slowly up to heat – until the jars are too hot to touch – and then turn off the heat.

8 Continue simmering and stirring until the whole mixture begins to thicken. When the consistency of the mixture is as described in the recipe, turn off the heat, and place the jars on a wooden surface or on newspaper.

9 Use the jug, mug or ladle and funnel to fill the jars so that the mixture is just short of the rim. Check that the rims fit the covers and store in a cool, dark place.

SPECIAL TIPS

• **Hot and dangerous:** It is always good if the children want to watch and learn, but they must be sitting down well away from the cooking and pouring activities. It is vital that you wear solid shoes – no bare feet or sandals – just in case you spill the hot mixture down your apron and onto your feet.

• **Balanced ingredients:** You can change the ingredients to suit your taste, but you must more or less stay with the basic amounts of vinegar and sugar.

• **Warm surface:** For safety's sake, when you are filling the jars, it is best to have them on a warm wooden surface – rather than cold tiles – so that the jars do not slip or suffer from thermal shock and crack.

If it is too thin

If, at the end of all your boiling and simmering, the chutney is too thin, you have either added too much vinegar, or you have under-weighed the sugar and/or the fruit and vegetable ingredients. Continue simmering and stirring to reduce the water.

If it is too thick

If the chutney is overly thick and treacly, you have probably over-weighed the sugar, and/or not added enough vinegar, and maybe also reduced the liquid content to the point where the sugar has started to caramelize. Add water little by little, and return the mixture to the heat, stirring constantly to make sure that the mixture does not burn.

CHUTNEY RECIPES

Green tomato chutney
A traditional recipe – a great way of using up unripe tomatoes – a good strong flavoured country chutney. The initial chopping decides the character of the chutney; if you like it chunky dice the tomatoes, but if you prefer it like a thick sauce pass it through a food processor.

Ingredients:
• 450 g (1 lb) cooking apples (Bramleys are best)
• 1.8 kg (4 lb) green tomatoes
• 450 g (1 lb) onions
• 225 g (8 oz) sultanas
• 570 ml (1 pint) vinegar
• 1 teaspoon salt
• 1 teaspoon mustard
• 1 teaspoon root ginger (in a bag)
• 1 teaspoon cayenne pepper
• 450 g (1 lb) brown sugar

Method:
1 Peel, core and chop the apples, dropping them in a bowl of water as you go to keep their colour. Drain and weigh them after preparation.
2 Wash and chop the tomatoes and weigh them after preparation.
3 Peel and chop the onions.
4 Put everything in the pan except the sugar and some of the vinegar, and simmer until the fruit is soft.
5 Dissolve the sugar in the vinegar and add to the mixture.
6 Simmer with the lid off, stirring constantly until the consistency is of thick jam.
7 Fill the jars and seal them.

Apple and onion chutney
This is the perfect way of using up a glut of apples and onions. The recipe can also easily be adapted to make a sauce; pass the ingredients through a food processor, add 28 g (1 oz) butter, and cut back slightly on the vinegar.

Ingredients:
• 1.8 kg (4 lb) cooking apples (Bramleys are best)
• 900 g (2 lb) onions
• 1 teaspoon salt
• 1 teaspoon mustard
• 1 teaspoon ground ginger
• 1 teaspoon cayenne pepper
• 1.7 litres (3 pints) vinegar
• 1.3 kg (3 lb) brown sugar

Method:
1 Peel, core and chop the apples, dropping them in a bowl of water as you go to keep their colour. Drain and weigh them after preparation.
2 Wash and chop the onions, and weigh them after preparation.
3 Put everything in the pan except the sugar and some of the vinegar, and simmer until the fruit is soft.
4 Dissolve the sugar in the vinegar and add to the mixture.
5 Simmer with the lid off, stirring constantly until the consistency is of thick jam.
6 Fill the jars and seal them.

Drying food

A couple of generations ago, from autumn through to spring, farmhouse kitchen ceilings were bedecked with strings of onions, chains of apple rings, bundles of herbs, cheeses and all manner of fish, fruit, meat and vegetables, all hanging up to dry. Drying is an excellent way of preserving certain foods for use during the lean winter months, and is very straightforward for onions, garlic, herbs and mushrooms.

What is the point of drying?

Health warning

If you make a mistake when drying herbs or onions, you will just finish up with a nasty taste in your mouth. It is not so simple, however, if you go wrong with fish or meat – you could well finish up in hospital or even worse. If you want to dry fish and meat – and this can be both exciting and rewarding in terms of experience and taste – you must seek advice from a specialist who is prepared to give you hands-on guidance.

POPULAR ITEMS FOR DRYING

- **Apples:** very easy and straight-forward; the 'leathery' slices are good as a snack.

- **Apricots:** a good option if you live in a sunny climate.

- **Bananas:** these may seem a funny choice, but they are good when there is a glut and huge quantities can be purchased at giveaway prices.

- **Herbs:** the easiest option and good for general flavouring of dishes.

- **Mushrooms:** easy and uncomplicated and the results are safe and predictable; they are good in stews.

- **Nuts:** wild nuts, such as chestnuts and cobnuts, can simply be gathered and spread out to dry.

- **Onions:** dried sliced onions are good for cooking.

- **Tomatoes:** these can either be halved and dried, or skinned, reduced to a pulp and then dried and flaked.

Drying mushrooms

Take your selected mushrooms, cut off the stems, peel the caps and inspect them to make sure they are in good condition. If they are small leave them as they are; otherwise, depending upon thickness, slice them into quarters or strips. Spread the prepared mushrooms over a stainless-steel rack and dry them in a very cool oven (50°C or 122°F). Alternatively, spread them on a wooden frame covered with cheesecloth or nylon netting and dry them in a purpose-made drier or on a rack near a wood-burning stove or range. Inspect the mushrooms at regular intervals and turn as necessary. Cool and store them in small individual airtight containers.

↗ *Carefully spread the sliced mushrooms over the rack.*

Drying onions and garlic

Take your carefully selected onions or garlic, remove the peel, check them over to make sure they are in good condition, and slice and dice. Spread the prepared onions or garlic on a rack in much the same way as the mushrooms (see above). You can either store them as little crispy bits in airtight containers, or you can further grind the crispy bits in a food processor, and dry and store them as powder. The idea of storing in lots of little containers is that you can avoid spoiling a bulk supply by repeatedly opening and closing.

↗ *Use a stainless-steel knife to slice and dice the onions.*

Drying herbs

On a sunny day, pick your herbs in the late morning when the sun has burned off the dew. Pick sprigs or leaves depending upon the herb, check them over, and remove any damaged bits. Tie them in a paper bag and hang them up in a warm, dry place – from the kitchen ceiling, for example, or near a stove or oven. When the herbs are absolutely crisp-dry, scrunch them up in the bag, remove any stalks, and pour the scrunched-up pieces into small airtight containers – one container for each little batch of herbs. Label and date the containers and store in a dry, dark cupboard. See also page 61 for tips on storing.

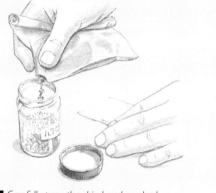

↗ *Carefully pour the dried and crushed herbs into clean, dry containers.*

Drying carrots

Take your carefully chosen carrots, throw away anything that looks in any way damaged, and wash, peel and dice. Take the pieces, and blanch them to destroy the enzymes that are responsible for spoilage – either by putting them in a net and dipping them in boiling water for about a minute, or by putting them in a stainless steel colander and steaming for about two minutes. When the blanching is complete, spread the diced carrots over a cheesecloth- or net-covered rack and dry as for mushrooms (see page 66). When the drying is complete, store the dried carrots in airtight containers and put them in a cool, dry, dark place. In the weeks and months between drying and usage, check them regularly to make sure they are dry and free from mould.

↗ *Swiftly blanch the diced carrots prior to drying.*

Drying bananas

Having purchased a bumper load of bargain bananas (low-cost because of a glut in the market), take your carefully chosen fruit and check them over to make sure that they are in good firm condition. Skin and remove any squidgy bits. Slice thinly or quarter along their length, and spread them out on a cheesecloth- or net-covered rack, and dry as for mushrooms (see page 66). At the end of the drying period, put the leathery slices in airtight containers, and store in a cool, dry, dark place.

↗ *Store the dry bananas in a clean, dry, airtight container.*

Drying tomatoes

Take your fully ripe tomatoes, remove damaged bits, and wash and quarter. Blanch for 3–4 minutes, and remove the skins and pips. Put the tomatoes through a food processor, and into a cheesecloth or net jelly bag. When the juice or water has drained off, spread the remaining pulp out over a plate and dry it as for mushrooms (see page 66). Finally, take the resultant flakes of dried tomatoes and store them in airtight containers.

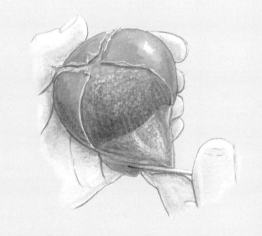

↗ *Blanch the tomatoes and then carefully peel off the skins.*

Smoking food

Why do we smoke food?

While smoking was traditionally a process of preserving food, it is now primarily a process of flavouring, and to some extent cooking. The process involves exposing the food – usually meat, fish or cheese – to wood smoke. When smoking your own food at home, it is best to start with cheese, and progress to salted fish and meat, before smoking fresh fish and meat, simply because cheese and salted fish and meat are less likely to go bad.

HEALTH ISSUES

Is smoked food a health risk? The facts, figures and evidence suggest that there is some risk if it is eaten in considerable quantities. The problem is that all smoked food – cheese, meat and fish – contains hydrocarbons which are known carcinogens. The reality, however, is that most of us never do eat, and never could eat, enough smoked food for this to be a concern.

HOT SMOKING

Hot smoking is a process that involves smoking food for a short time at high temperatures in a confined container – a bit like a barbecue. The temperatures reach 50–80°C (122–176°F), and are high enough to cook the food and destroy all the microbes.

COLD SMOKING

Cold smoking is a process that involves housing the food in a smokehouse – a shed, hut or room – and filling the room with smoke so that the room temperature reaches 15–25°C (59–77°F). While the smoke gives the food a protective coating, and to some degree destroys the surface microbes, the food is still uncooked, and the microbes within the food are alive and well. Traditionally, the potential dangers of this process are avoided by salting the food before it is smoked.

Warning

If smoked fish or meat looks in any way as if the texture is breaking down, has a sticky texture, is giving off an unpleasant smell, or has an unpleasant taste, then throw it away.

Cold smoking cheese

You need 900 g (2 lb) of hard cheese, the use of a smoke cabinet, charcoal, and apple wood or a similar fruit wood in the form of sawdust. Having air-dried the cheese for about an hour, put it in the top of the cabinet, and light the charcoal. When the charcoal is well alight, heap it over with the sawdust and close the door. Keep tending the fire so as to achieve maximum smoke and minimum temperature. When the smoking is complete really depends upon your taste; try a little sample every hour or so until you like the taste.

↗ *If the cheese looks overly hot, then either raise the shelf or damp the fire.*

Hot smoking fish

You need 2.2 litres (4 pints) of fresh water, a cup of salt, half a cup of brown sugar, the juice of one lemon, a teaspoonful each of garlic powder, onion powder and black pepper, and about 450 g (1 lb) of fresh prepared fish – something like herrings or mackerel. In a glass, plastic or stainless-steel container, mix together the water, salt, lemon juice, garlic, onion and pepper. Place the prepared fresh fish in the liquid and leave it to soak – allow about an hour for every 450 g (1 lb). At the end of the allotted period, remove the fish, set it on a wooden rack, cover it with cheesecloth and put it in a cool, breezy place. After about an hour, when a glazed coating has formed on the fish, put it in the smoker in the same way as for cheese (see above). The smoking is complete when the fish comes away as firm, dry flakes. Finally, either eat the fish as it comes from the smoker, or keep it in a fridge for no more than four weeks.

↗ *Soak the prepared fish in the liquid.*

Curing and cold smoking bacon

You need two large slabs of boned-out belly pork, a 23 kg (50 lb) bag of salt, half a cup of brown sugar, black pepper, an eggcupful of saltpetre, a large, shallow, waterproof, wooden washtub or shallow plastic storage box long enough to take the pork when it is set flat down, enough fine-weave muslin to double-wrap both slabs of pork separately, a large bodkin-type needle and strong linen thread.

Take the pork (five days after it has been killed) and trim off all loose bits. Pour a thick layer of salt into the bottom of the box/tub and set one slab skin-side down. Rub a pinch or two of the saltpetre into the uppermost surface of the meat. Set the second slab on top of the first and repeat the procedure. Set the two slabs together so that the skin sides are outermost, bury the whole thing in the salt, and leave in a cool place overnight. Next morning, pour off the liquid, make sure there is plenty of salt between the two slabs, and once again bury it all in salt.

↗ Thoroughly rub in the saltpetre and the salt.

After a week or so, when there is no more liquid to pour off, remove the sides, brush away the salt, loosely wrap them in the muslin, and hang them up in a cool, draughty place to air-dry. After about two weeks, when the part-cured bacon feels dry to the touch, take it one slab at a time, double-wrap it in the muslin, and sew it up so as to make a parcel.

After about nine months, when the bacon feels rock hard, remove the covering and hang the bacon in a small brick building – the smokehouse. Place a wood-burning stove against the outside of the smokehouse, with the chimney going through the wall, and start burning fruit or oak wood. Keep the fire going for 24 hours and the job is finished.

↗ Double wrap with muslin and sew it up.

A top-quality smoker is a good option if you want to do more than dabble with smoking.

This shows how the food to be smoked is arranged in relationship to the source of smoke.

Top lid handle

Transport handle

Top shelf and rack

Viewing door

Middle shelf

Water pan

Charcoal fire

Fire base

Making beer

Is brewing complicated?

If you intend to use all your own raw ingredients, it will be more complicated, in that when something goes wrong – and it usually does the first time around – you will not know for sure which element or sequence is at fault. The best advice for beginners is to use your own hops plus shop-bought grains and malt, and then later, when you more fully understand your needs, to change over to using all your own carefully sourced ingredients.

Nothing imparts a fine fresh hop aroma like good-quality whole hops.

THE INGREDIENTS

In essence, beer is made from water, barley, yeast and hops; the amounts vary depending upon the type of beer being made. Traditionally, the barley is soaked in warm water for 3–4 days, drained and spread for 10 days or so until the grains have chitted (meaning until each grain of barley has sprouted a shoot), dried, roasted and cracked, boiled with water and hops, mixed with yeast, fermented, and finally racked into bottles or barrels.

As to what type of beer you want to make, and how many bought-in ingredients you want to use, much will depend on what you are producing in the way of ingredients. For example, you may have barley, yeast and hops, and be prepared to work through all the procedures; if, however, you can only supply the hops, and/or you want to speed up and miss out soaking and chitting the barley, then you can buy in ready-made crushed grains, liquid malt and so on.

BASIC BEER-MAKING EQUIPMENT

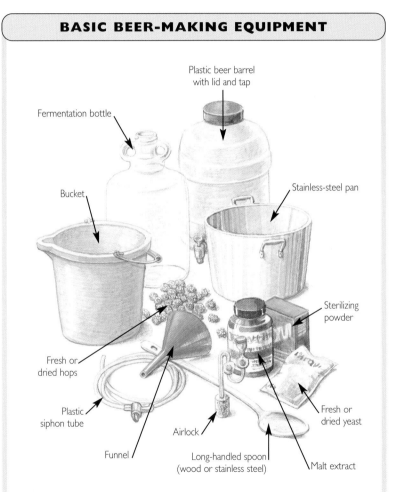

Plastic beer barrel with lid and tap

Fermentation bottle

Bucket

Stainless-steel pan

Sterilizing powder

Fresh or dried hops

Plastic siphon tube

Airlock

Fresh or dried yeast

Funnel

Long-handled spoon (wood or stainless steel)

Malt extract

The beer-making kit illustrated above is based on the premise that, apart from the hops, you are going buy in yeast, crushed grains and malt extract in liquid or powder form, boil ingredients in the pan, manage the fermentation in a glass bottle, and rack the resultant beer in a plastic barrel. The size of the pan and the size and number of bottles and barrels will depend upon just how much beer you have in mind to make. You will also need a heat source, a good amount of space and the use of various tables and surfaces.

BASIC BEER-MAKING METHODS

1 Put 7 litres (about 12 pints) of water on to heat.
2 Put your shop-bought crushed grains in a muslin straining bag and soak them in the slowly heating water for about 15–20 minutes.
3 At the end of the allotted time, before the water is boiling, stir and press the grains and remove them from the water.
4 Once the water has come to the boil, turn off the heat, let it sit for five minutes, and then stir in the malt extract.
5 Bring the liquid back up to the boil, all the time stirring the mix and being careful that it does not burn or boil over.
6 Take your hops, all nicely contained in the muslin straining bag, and drop them into the simmering mix.
7 Simmer for about an hour, and then turn off the heat and cool the pan in a sink of cold water.
8 Once the mix has cooled, pour it into the fermentation bottle and top it up with enough cold drinking water to bring it to the 23-litre (about 5-gallon) mark on the bottle.
9 Take the yeast, mix it as directed, pour it into the bottle and fit the airlock.
10 Having watched the foam rise to a head and then settle and flatten down (this will take about five days), remove the airlock and siphon the beer into the barrel.

Syphon

SPECIAL TIPS

Experiment: It is always a good to try new ideas, the proviso being that you keep notes. If you are given hops or would like to add a dash of herbs, for example, then have a go. Of course, if you have kept notes, and you come up with a wonder beer, then you can make some more.

Health and safety: Always make sure that the equipment has been sterilized; there should be no dust or bits from a previous brewing. Use plastic barrels rather than bottles, so that you do not have to worry about bottles exploding.

Clubs: Beer-making and real-ale clubs are a great idea; join in with a beer-making session.

Jargon: Beer-making is beset with words such as sparging, flooring, spreeing, wort, mashing, dumping, pitching and many more besides. It is good to use them, but not until you know what you are talking about.

If it tastes good

This is wonderful, but only if you have made detailed notes so that you can make more of the same. Every aspect is critical – the source of the water, room temperature, the shape of the vessels, and so on.

If it tastes bad

The chances are that one of the ingredients was at fault or the beer was attacked by harmful bacteria. If it tastes really vinegary, open it up to the air and let it go the whole way, so that you have vinegar rather than beer.

BEER RECIPES

Basic small mead
A traditional honey mead, ready to drink in eight weeks, best served chilled

Ingredients:
• 3 slices ginger
• 3 cloves
• 2 sticks cinnamon
• 1 slice orange peel
• 900 g (2 lb) honey
• small packet yeast
• ¼ cup grain alcohol (such as vodka)

Method:
1 Boil and simmer the ginger, cloves, cinnamon and orange peel in 4.5 litres (8 pints) of water.
2 Top up with another 3.5 litres (6 pints) of water, bring to a simmer, and stir in the honey.
3 Spoon off the scum, remove from the heat, cover, and leave overnight.
4 Add the yeast, syphon the mixture into a jar, fit an airlock and ferment for two days.
5 Add the grain alcohol, pour the mixture into a barrel and ferment for eight weeks.

Wheat beer
A strong, refreshing lager

Ingredients:
• 1.8 kg (4 lb) wheat beer extract
• 2 cups organic brown sugar
• 28 g (1 oz) Saaz hops
• Packet Wyeast ale yeast

Method:
1 Bring 9 litres (16 pints) of water to the boil and add the wheat beer extract and the sugar.
2 Add two-thirds of the hops and simmer for 30 minutes.
3 Remove from the heat and add the rest of the hops.
4 Top up with water to make 18 litres (32 pints).
5 Cool and add the yeast.
6 Ferment and siphon into a barrel.

American pale ale
A characteristic ale flavour, light and lemony

Ingredients:
• 450 g (1 lb) Cara-pils malt
• 3 kg (7 lb) light unhopped syrup
• 28 g (1 oz) Hallertauer hops (pellets)
• 1 teaspoon Irish moss
• dash salt
• dash citric acid
• 2 teaspoons yeast nutrient
• 2 packs Munton yeast

Method:
1 Put the malt into 9 litres (16 pints) of water, bring to the boil and simmer for an hour.
2 Add more boiling water to bring it up to 17 litres (30 pints), and add the syrup and half of the hops.
3 Simmer and add the Irish moss and the rest of the hops.
4 Simmer for an hour and add all the remaining ingredients except the yeast.
5 Top up with water to make 23 litres (40 pints) and add the yeast.
6 Ferment and siphon into a barrel.

Making cider

Is cider-making as easy as it sounds?

Cider almost makes itself. You can make a very successful basic rough cider simply by putting any old apples in a plastic bucket, pounding them with a wooden cudgel, pouring the juice into a barrel, and fitting an airlock – nature will do the rest. If you are more selective with the apples, however, and if you invest in a small press, you will be able to make more cider in half the time. The type of press illustrated here is the best of the best.

Gathering apples in the sunshine can be one of life's greatest pleasures.

THE INGREDIENTS

The wonderful thing about cider is its essential simplicity – just apples and water. Of course, the quality of the cider will depend upon the variety of apple, the character of the growing year, the type and number of yeasts that naturally occur on the apples, and time spent on the various procedures, and some people do destroy the natural yeast and add their own yeast, but in essence cider is just about apples. Even better, the preparation could not be more direct. You just collect windfall apples, throw away anything that is obviously squashy or diseased, and that is it. No worrying about wormholes, or peeling and coring, or even washing if the orchard is clean with long grass. A good cider apple should be very juicy and tart. I like Russet, Baldwin and Newton, but some cider-makers favour varieties like Winesap, Gravenstein and Roxbury. Experiment with your own apples, and see what happens.

BASIC CIDER-MAKING EQUIPMENT

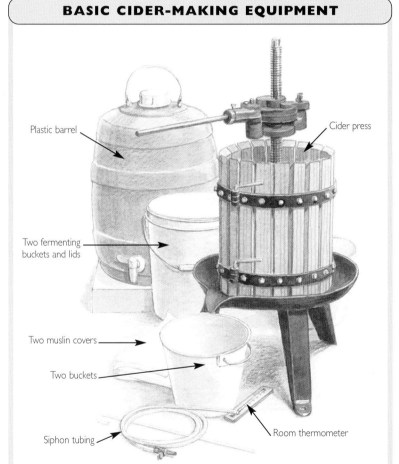

Plastic barrel

Cider press

Two fermenting buckets and lids

Two muslin covers

Two buckets

Siphon tubing

Room thermometer

The cider-making kit illustrated above is based on the premise that you are going to make natural cider, using clean windfalls from a clean, grassy orchard, that you are going to rely on the natural yeasts as they occur on the apples, and that you have the use of a well-stocked kitchen. You need a press, juicer or liquidizer to turn the apples into pulp, a couple of plastic buckets, two 23-litre (5-gallon) fermenting buckets complete with lids, two pieces of fine-weave muslin large enough to cover the buckets, a room thermometer, a 23-litre (5-gallon) plastic barrel complete with airlock, and a simple siphon complete with tubing.

BASIC CIDER-MAKING METHOD

Siphon

1 Gather your fully ripe, nicely bruised windfall apples from a clean, grassy, meadow orchard. Check them over and throw away anything that is rotten. Do not worry about bruises, wormholes and bloomy, yeasty skins – it all adds character.

2 Crush, press, grind or beat the apples and collect the juice in the buckets.

3 Pour the juice into the fermentation buckets – three-quarters fill one bucket, and go on to the next.

4 Cover the buckets with the muslin, tie it around with string, and loosely sit the lids in place.

5 Hold the room temperature at a comfortable level – about 15–21°C (60–70°F).

6 Being careful not dislodge the muslin, check several times a day – just to make sure that it is nicely bubbling without overflowing.

7 Once the brew has settled down and the bubbles have flattened out, siphon the cider into the barrel and fit the airlock.

Warning

Never use glass bottles – they could explode and cause serious injury. It is easier, cheaper and safer to use plastic barrels rather than bottles.

SPECIAL TIPS

• **New ideas:** It is always good to try new ideas. If a cider-making neighbour says that he does it in a certain way, or he would use different equipment, give it a try and see what happens.

• **A second crushing:** Traditionally, some cider-makers used to make a second crushing – that is, they passed the apples through the press and took away the juice for first-quality cider, and they mixed the pulp from the first pressing with water, left it overnight, and recrushed for second-quality cider.

If it tastes good

If your cider tastes good one year, everything has been just right – a good apple variety, just the right growing conditions, the correct amount of juice, a perfect yeast and successful procedures. It is important to keep notes, or better still a diary, so that you can repeat everything the next time around. If you have used half your apples and half from a neighbour, or if you did one procedure a different way around, it is vital that you have it on record.

If it tastes bad

If your cider tastes a bit vinegary, the chances are that the dreaded vinegar fly has got through the muslin. The best you can do at this stage is make the best of a bad job and use the cider vinegar for cooking, and make another batch of cider.

RECIPES USING CIDER

Mid-winter mulled apple cider

A traditional winter drink. If you want to make a dramatic entrance, miss out the saucepan, take a poker from a hot fire and plunge it into the mixture. The mixture will splash and splutter, so make sure that everyone is out of harm's way.

Ingredients:
• 10 cups cider
• half a cup dark brown sugar
• 2 sticks cinnamon
• 10 cloves
• juice of one lemon
• juice of one orange

Method:
1 Tie the spices into a screwed-up piece of cheesecloth.
2 Put all the ingredients into a large heat-resistant glass, jug or bowl.
3 Stir the ingredients with a wooden spoon.
4 Pour the ingredients into a saucepan and gently simmer for 15 minutes.
5 Finally, remove the spices and pour the mulled cider into mugs.

Baked apples with cider sauce

This is a traditional farmhouse pudding that children will like.

Ingredients:
• 4 large apples
• 2 dessertspoons raisins
• 8 almonds
• 4 teaspoons marmalade
• 4 teaspoons brown sugar
• 4 teaspoons butter
• 1 cup water
• 1 cup cider
• 1 tablespoon of cornflower
• vanilla ice cream

Method:
1 Wash and core the apples, makin sure you remove every last bit of core.
2 Fill each apple with nuts, marmalade, sugar and butter.
3 Place the apples in a medium hot oven.
4 After about 25–55 minutes, when the apples are soft, stir the cider and cornflower together in a saucepan and cook until thick.
5 To serve, sit the apple in cider sauce, and bury it under a heap of ice cream.

Ice-cream cider

A beautiful, refreshing, long, cool drink that is just the thing for a summer treat.

Ingredients:
• 2.2 litres (4 pints) chilled cider
• 4 generous portions home-made vanilla ice cream
• 4 teaspoons home-made strawberry jam or syrup
• 4 tablespoons chopped almonds

Method:
1 Set up four glasses, each three-quarters full of chilled cider.
2 Spoon out the ice cream and float it on the cider.
3 Dribble the jam or syrup over the ice cream, heap almonds over the top, and serve immediately with a long spoon and a straw.

Making wine

Many people boast that they have made wine from coal, oak leaves, crushed beans and other strange ingredients, but why would you want to? In the knowledge that wine is best made from sugar-rich juice, it is so much easier to make it from common or garden juicy items like rhubarb, blackberries, elderberries, sloes, parsnips and sugar beet – something that you know from experience promises sweetness.

Pick the fruit for making the wine when it is ripe - while it is still crisp and clean and firm to the touch.

THE INGREDIENTS

Although in the past wine-making has sometimes been thought of as being complicated and exotic, it is really no more difficult to make than cider. You have the basic ingredient – the fruit, flowers, herbs or vegetables – and the water, sugar and yeast. The quality of the end product depends upon the basic ingredient, the character of the growing year, the type of yeast, and the time and effort spent on the various procedures. If you are a beginner, try a basic wine, see how it goes, and, when you have a better understanding of the whole process, start experimenting.

BASIC WINE-MAKING EQUIPMENT

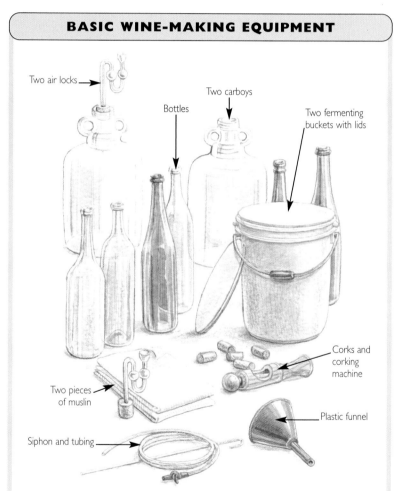

Two air locks

Two carboys

Bottles

Two fermenting buckets with lids

Corks and corking machine

Two pieces of muslin

Plastic funnel

Siphon and tubing

The illustration above shows a basic starting kit complete with bottles, the idea being that you intend to swap bottles of wine with wine-making friends and neighbours. You need two 23-litre (5-gallon) fermenting buckets with lids, two pieces of fine-weave muslin large enough to cover the buckets, two fermentation carboys complete with airlocks, a 23-litre (5-gallon) stainless-steel pan, a large plastic funnel, a siphon complete with tubing, as many empty wine bottles as you can find, new corks, a corking machine and the use of a well-equipped kitchen.

BASIC WINE-MAKING METHOD

1 Place the main ingredient – the washed and sliced fruit, flowers, herbs or vegetables – together with the sugar and water into a plastic fermenting bucket, tub or dustbin.
2 Pour boiling water over the ingredients.
3 Cool to lukewarm, and add the appropriate wine yeast.
4 Drape the piece of fine-weave muslin over the tub and tie it securely.
5 After the allotted time, when all the fuss and bubbles – meaning the primary fermentation – have more or less subsided, carefully siphon the liquid off into the carboys, fit airlocks and put in a dark room.
6 Once the secondary fermentation has taken place, carefully siphon the wine into the bottles and cork and cap them.

Siphon

SPECIAL TIPS

• **Sterilization:** It is vital, every step along the way, that you clean and sterilize the equipment. You must wash everything – all the tubs, bottles, tubs, spoons and jugs – with boiling water and/or sterilize it with a chemical. Most wine-making failures are caused by sloppy hygiene.

• **Plastic barrels versus bottles:** If you leave the wine in plastic barrels it will be easier and safer, and you will not be bothered by all the fuss of bottling, but you will not be able to give bottles away. It needs thinking about.

Warning

If you bottle the wine too early (before the secondary fermentation has subsided) and/or you add too much sugar, the bottles could explode and cause serious injury. Some people like to rack the wine (meaning siphon it from one carboy to another) several times before finally bottling it.

WINE RECIPES

Plum wine

Ingredients:
• 1.8 kg (4 lb) plums, stoned and quartered
• 900 g (2 lb) sugar
• 4.5 litres (1 gallon) pure water
• Burgundy yeast

Method:
1 Place the plums and 225 g (8 oz) sugar into the fermentation bucket and cover with the boiling water.
2 When the mixture has cooled, add the yeast according to the instructions on the packet.
3 After a day or so, when the initial fermentation has flattened out, add another 225 g (8 oz) of sugar.
4 After 3–4 weeks, add another 225 g (8 oz) of sugar, and 3–4 weeks later the last 225 g (8 oz).
5 When the primary fermentation has ceased, carefully siphon into carboys and fit airlocks.
6 Finally bottle the wine.

Rhubarb wine

Ingredients:
• 2.2 kg (5 lb) prepared rhubarb – washed and trimmed
• 1.3–1.8 kg (3–4 lb) sugar
• 4.5 litres (1 gallon) pure water
• mugful raisins
• 2 oranges, chopped and sliced
• 2 lemons, chopped and sliced
• 28 g (1 oz) yeast
• 1 slice thick brown toast

Method:
1 Cut the rhubarb into short lengths.
2 Put it in the fermentation tub, add the sugar, stir, cover and leave overnight.
3 Boil the water, pour it over the mixture and cover.
4 Stir and re-cover every day for a week.
5 Strain the liquid through a muslin cloth into a pan, and heat it to just short of boiling point.
6 Pour the hot liquid back into the tub and add the raisins, oranges and lemons.
7 Mix the yeast as directed on the packet, spread it over the toast, float the toast on the liquid, and cover.
8 Remove the toast when the primary fermentation has flattened out.
9 After about 2–3 weeks, siphon into carboy and fit an airlock. Resiphon into a fresh carboy once a month for three months, and then bottle.

Blackberry wine

Ingredients:
• 9-litre (2-gallon) bucket of blackberries, topped, tailed and washed
• 9 litres (2 gallons) water
• 3.6 kg (8 lb) sugar
• Burgundy yeast
• 1 slice thick brown toast

Method:
1 Put the blackberries in the tub and mash them to a pulp.
2 Boil the water, pour it over the mixture, cover and leave overnight.
3 Strain the liquid through a muslin cloth and heat it to just short of boiling point.
4 Pour the hot liquid back into the tub and add the sugar.
5 Mix the yeast as directed on the packet, spread it over the toast, float the toast on the liquid, and cover.
6 After about a week, remove the remains of the toast.
7 After about 2–3 weeks, siphon into a carboy and fit an airlock.
8 Resiphon into a fresh carboy every month for three months, and bottle the wine when it is clear.

Making vegetarian soap

How easy is it to make soap?

Traditionally, soap was made from a mixture of animal fat – not so good if you are a vegetarian or vegan – and lye (sodium hydroxide). There is now a lot of interest in making vegetarian soaps from pure plant oils such as cocoa fat or olive oil. Make sure when you are getting the ingredients that they are labelled 'organic – free from toxins and animal products'. Be sure to read the labels carefully, because chemical products are being sold as 'eco-friendly'.

EQUIPMENT AND INGREDIENTS

You need a large stainless-steel pan, the use of a well-stocked kitchen complete with jugs, scales and a thermometer, a kit of coverall clothes complete with goggles and elbow-length gloves, clean old blanket (or similar), a large shallow metal, plastic or wooden tray, a roll of plastic wrap, dried herbs of your choice, 28 g (1 oz) pure cocoa butter, 200g (7 oz) pure olive oil, 200g (7 oz) pure white coconut oil, 450 g (1 lb) pure vegetarian shortening, 340 g (12 oz) rainwater, and 115 g (4 oz) lye (sodium hydroxide).

> ### Warning
> Lye (sodium hydroxide) burns. Treat it with extreme caution, just like acid.

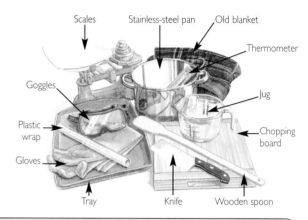

Scales • Stainless-steel pan • Old blanket • Thermometer • Goggles • Jug • Plastic wrap • Chopping board • Gloves • Tray • Knife • Wooden spoon

STEP-BY-STEP METHOD

1 Spread the blanket over your work surface, line the tray with the plastic wrap and put it on the blanket. Put the cocoa butter, olive oil, coconut oil and shortening into the pan, make sure that you can work undisturbed, and don your protective gear ready for action.

2 Put the pan on a very low heat, bring the temperature up to a maximum of 48°C (120°F) and turn off the heat.

3 Very carefully, pour the pure water into a jug, followed by the lye, and stir. When the oil mixture in the pan has cooled to 37°C (100°F), very carefully add the lye and stir in your chosen herbs.

4 When the mixture has cooled to a thick but still runny consistency, pour it into the tray, cover it with plastic, and carefully fold the edges of the blanket up and over to cover it. After 24–36 hours, slice the soap into hand-sized bars.

Making candles

Candles can be made in many different ways. They can be pressed, like 'tea lights'; they can be cast, like most commercially made candles; they can be wrapped, like candles made from sheets of beeswax; they can be dipped, like old English cottage-type candles; and they can be made from a mixture of the above techniques, as described below. The procedure below draws its inspiration from traditional Japanese techniques for making ceremonial temple candles.

What do I need to make candles?

EQUIPMENT AND INGREDIENTS

You need a double-boiler type of saucepan (such as a porringer or a woodworker's glue pot), a pair of long-nosed pliers, a wooden cutting board, a sharp craft-type knife, a metal ruler, scissors, a roll of cotton wick suitable for 2.5 cm (1 in) diameter candles, a 450 g (1 lb) block of beeswax, one sheet of flat, honeycomb-patterned beeswax about 30 cm (12 in) square for every dozen candles that you want to make, the use of a well-equipped kitchen, and a set of coverall clothes.

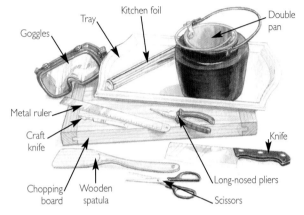

Kitchen foil
Tray
Goggles
Double pan
Metal ruler
Craft knife
Knife
Chopping board
Wooden spatula
Long-nosed pliers
Scissors

> **Warning**
>
> *Hot wax is dangerous. Wear protective clothing and make sure that you can work undisturbed.*

STEP-BY-STEP METHOD

1 Cut the block of wax into flakes and put it in the double boiler to heat.

2 Use the scissors to cut one 31.5 cm (12½ in) length of wick for each candle that you want to make, and use the knife to cut the wax sheet into 12 strips, 2.5 cm (1 in) wide.

3 Use the pliers to drop the wick into the wax, stir it around for a few seconds, lift it clear and then put it on one side to go hard.

4 Take a primed wick, arrange it along one edge of a wax strip so that one end protrudes by about 1.5 cm (½ in), and use your fingertips to roll a tight taper. Take a wax-covered taper, dip it into the melted wax, first one end and then the other, and use your fingertips to compact the wax. Repeat this dipping and rolling until the candle is about 1.5 cm (½ in) in diameter.

Glossary

Alternative energy home A home that uses non-fossil energy.

Autonomous The ability to function independently of other components or systems, the state of being independent and self contained. In the context of this book, the term is used to describe houses and to some extent social groups, that are self sufficient in terms of energy and food. The term "Autonomous House" relates to the book "The Autonomous House" by Robert and Brenda Vale.

Cobbett William Cobbett, born in England in 1763 was a writer, MP, philosopher, and free thinker. In 1821 he wrote "Cottage Economy" a book that describes in detail how to achieve "family happiness" by becoming self-sufficient, or as Cobbett so nicely put it… "A good living". If you want to know in detail how to brew beer, make bread, keep pigs, geese, ducks, bees and all the rest, then this is a good book to go for.

Earth ships A term used to describe self contained low impact homes.

Ecology The study of the relationships between living organisms and their environment – the whole works…humans, plants, animals, the earth – the study of how animals, plants, are affected by, and or interact with the environment.

Ecologically balanced Meaning a home and way of life that is ecologically responsible.

Eco-friendly Not harmful or threatening to the environment. Such and such group, way of life, object or system might be described as eco-friendly. To some extent the term has been rubbished/weakened/emasculated by advertisers who use it to describe everything from washing powders through to tee shirts.

Eco self-sufficiency A term used to describe a home and way of life that is in tune with nature.

Eco-warrior A term used to describe a certain type of environmental activist or crusader. Eco-warriors are usually portrayed by the medium as being long haired hippy tree-hugging Robin Hood type figures.

Environmentally friendly A home and way of living that is in tune with the environment.

Fossil fuels Hydrocarbon deposits formed underground from the remains of dead plants and animals – oil, natural gas and coal – fuels derived from living matter from previous geological time. Supplies of fossil fuels are fast running out.

Green A term used to describe people, systems, groups and ideas that are thought to be eco-friendly.

Green-dreamers A term used to describe people who yearn to become self-sufficient. The term was used back in the 1960's to describe hippy type groups who wanted to drop out and go back to the land.

Grid Although the term was originally used to describe the power utilities – gas, electricity and water – simply because these companies actually used grids of cables and pipes to feed our homes, the term is now also used in a general way to describe other energy sources that are easily distributed. So for example if you use oil and coal then you are also to some extent on the grid.

Grid-linked Or grid tie-in - describes homes that are dependent on the power utilities. Most people in developed countries are grid-linked.

Hippy A hippy or hippie is a person who rejects many of the standards and conventions of the society in which they live. For the most part the term is used by the establishment to negatively describe people who they think are anti-establishment. Many 60's hippy communes set out to become self-sufficient.

New age A term used to describe people, groups, concepts that draw inspiration from a broad range of religions and philosophies. To some extent New Age is an extension or reworking of Hippy.

Off-grid A term used to describe houses in the developed world that by necessity or choice source their own water and energy. A house in town is on-grid, while a house out in the country – up in the mountains or away in the forest is off-grid. The term is also now used to describe an independent way of life. While off-grid is also sometimes described as "unplugged" – meaning not connected to the utilities – the term is also used in a hippy sense to describe people who choose to "turn off".

On-grid See Grid-linked

Passive A house that used natural phenomena to set systems in motion – hot air rises, black surfaces absorb heat, white surfaces reflect heat, hot water rises. A passive system works without the need for motors, fans, blowers and the like.

Renewable energy Renewable energy, sometimes also termed sustainable energy, relates to all non fossil energy. So for example… wind energy, solar energy, geothermal energy, biomass energy is all renewable.

Self-Sufficiency A self contained multi system of living that involves producing food, creating energy and recycling waste without recourse to outside agencies. Self-sufficiency has been described as "subsistence plus cream". A truly self-sufficient set-up would grow all its own food – plants and animals – trade excess produce, create its own energy, and manage its own waste. In the context of this book, while self-sufficiency isn't necessarily achievable, it is the target to aim for.

Thoreau Henry David Thoreau – born in America in 1817, was an author, naturalist and philosopher. In 1847 he set out on a two-year experiment in simple back-to-nature living. He built a little hut on the edge of Walden Pond. "Walden" is his account of solitary, self-sufficient living. Though at the time of writing the book was thought of as cranky – lots of talk about building huts, fishing, eating beans, spreading manure, living off the land, not minding about patched clothes and such – it is now considered to be "a classic American book… a spiritual quest… a book that explores natural simplicity and harmony, a book that questions everything about our economic and ecological environment".

Trombe wall Named after its inventor Felix Trombe – is a passive solar heating and ventilation system that is made up of a masonry wall covered in glass. In action… the sun shines through the glass, the wall absorbs heat, and the space between the glass and the wall becomes a thermal chimney. The resultant hot air within the thermal chimney is directed and channelled by natural convection either into the building - so that it heats the interior – or out of the building – so that it cools the interior. The joy of the Trombe system is that it can be operated without the need for complex electro mechanical systems – no fans, motors or blowers.

Index

ACKNOWLEDGEMENTS

We would like to thank the following for their help and advice, and for their photographs which appear in this book

ALTERNATIVE TECHNOLOGY

Centre for Alternative Technology (CAT)
Machynlleth, Powys SY20 9AZ, UK
Tel: 01654 705953
Fax: 01654 702782
Email: info@cat.org.uk
www.cat.org.uk
CAT is open all year round, seven days a week

BEEKEEPING

David Bates
www.honeyshop.co.uk
www.somersetbeekeepers.org.uk

Brushy Mountain Bee Farm
610 Bethany Church Road, Moravian Falls,
NC 28654, USA
Tel: 1-800-BEESWAX (1-800-233-7929)
www.brushymountainbeefarm.com

CATTLE

**Purebred Dexter Cattle Association
of North America**
25979 Highway EE, Prairie Home, Missouri,
USA 65068
Contact: Wes Patton, Glenn Land Farm,
Orland, California, USA
www.glennlandfarm.com

Shetland Cattle Breeders Association
Mary Holloway
Barnack, Langley, Liss, Hampshire
GU33 7JR, UK
Tel: 01730 895006
Email: info@shetlandcattle.org.uk
www.shetlandcattle.org.uk

GOATS AND OFF-GRID

**The Caldwell Family (Gianaclis and
Vern, and their multi-talented
daughter and goat partner Amelia)**
Pholia Farm, Nigerian Dwarf Dairy Goats
and Creamery, 9115 West Evans Cr. Road
Rogue River, Oregon, USA
www.pholiafarm.com

HOME BREWING

Peter Hood
The Brew Shop UK, 48 Buxton Rd,
Stockport SK2 6NB, UK
Tel: 0161 480 4880
www.thebrewshop.com
www.winepress4u.co.uk

PIGS

Richard Lutwyche
British Saddleback Breeders' Club, Dryft
Cottage, South Cerney, Cirencester
GL7 5UB, UK
Email: mail@saddlebacks.org.uk
www.saddlebacks.org.uk

POULTRY

Jason and Kerry Weller
Mantel Farm, Henley Down, Catsfield
Nr Battle, East Sussex, TN33 9BN, UK
Tel: 01424 830357

SMOKING FOOD

BBQ and Smoker Specialists
ProBBQ Ltd, 2 Clifden Road, St Austell,
Cornwall PL25 4NU, UK
Tel: 01726 76245
Fax: 01726 76246
www.probbq.co.uk

**WIND TURBINES
AND SOLAR POWER**

Dulas Ltd
Unit 1, Dyfi Eco Park, Machylleth, Powys
SY20 8AX, UK
Tel: 01654 705000
Fax: 01654 703000
Email: info@dulas.org.uk
www.dulas.org.uk
*Specialists in designing and supplying
photovoltaic (PV) sources, including grid-
connected integrated PV and water pumps*

Iskra Wind Turbines Ltd
Loughborough Innovation Centre, Epinal
Way, Loughborough LE11 3EH, UK
Tel: 0845 8380588
Email: enquiries@iskrawind.com
www.iskrawind.com